T0318497

Cambridge Elements ≡

Elements in Metaphysics
edited by
Tuomas E. Tahko
University of Bristol

DISPOSITIONS AND POWERS

Toby Friend
University of Bristol

Samuel Kimpton-Nye
University of Bristol

CAMBRIDGE
UNIVERSITY PRESS

Shaftesbury Road, Cambridge CB2 8EA, United Kingdom

One Liberty Plaza, 20th Floor, New York, NY 10006, USA

477 Williamstown Road, Port Melbourne, VIC 3207, Australia

314–321, 3rd Floor, Plot 3, Splendor Forum, Jasola District Centre,
New Delhi – 110025, India

103 Penang Road, #05–06/07, Visioncrest Commercial, Singapore 238467

Cambridge University Press is part of Cambridge University Press & Assessment,
a department of the University of Cambridge.

We share the University's mission to contribute to society through the pursuit of
education, learning and research at the highest international levels of excellence.

www.cambridge.org
Information on this title: www.cambridge.org/9781009113014

DOI: 10.1017/9781009118910

First published 2023

A catalogue record for this publication is available from the British Library.

ISBN 978-1-009-11301-4 Paperback
ISSN 2633-9862 (online)
ISSN 2633-9854 (print)

Dispositions and Powers

Elements in Metaphysics

DOI: 10.1017/9781009118910
First published online: March 2023

Toby Friend
University of Bristol

Samuel Kimpton-Nye
University of Bristol

Author for correspondence: Toby Friend, toby.friend@bristol.ac.uk

Abstract: As we understand them, dispositions are relatively uncontroversial 'predicatory' properties had by objects disposed in certain ways. By contrast, powers are hypothetical 'ontic' properties posited in order to explain dispositional behaviour. Section 1 outlines this distinction in more detail. Section 2 offers a summary of the issues surrounding analysis of dispositions and various strategies in contemporary literature to address them, including one of our own. Section 3 describes some of the important questions facing the metaphysics of powers, including why they are worth positing and how they might metaphysically explain laws of nature and modality. This title is also available as Open Access on Cambridge Core.

Keywords: analysis of dispositions, metaphysics of powers, laws of nature, modality, structural equations

ISBNs: 9781009113014 (PB), 9781009118910 (OC)
ISSNs: 2633-9862 (online), 2633-9854 (print)

Contents

1 Introduction

Insofar as they exist at all, both dispositions and powers are properties of objects. Moreover, they are both properties which concern how objects are disposed to behave. But there would be no point in writing an Element about dispositions *and* powers if the two kinds of property were obviously identical. Nor would there be much point in writing a single text about both if they were not closely related. In this introductory section we'll clarify what makes them distinct and, if powers theorists have things right, what relates them. Sections 2 and 3 then take a deeper dive into the issues surrounding our philosophical understanding of each kind of property.

Let's consider dispositions first. The topic of dispositions is an important one because they would seem to be pervasive in *science* (see, e.g., Ellis and Lierse 1994; Harre and Madden 1975);[1] and dispositions have been used to define concepts in a variety of different philosophical domains. Examples include dispositional definitions of *beliefs* (e.g., Ryle 1949; Schwitzgebel 2002), *values* (e.g., Brower 1993; Smith et al. 1989), and *knowledge* (e.g., Constantin 2018; Yalowitz 2000). As we intend to use the term, a *disposition* is a property of being disposed in some specific way. Among these we count so-called canonical (or 'overt') dispositions, which are denoted by phrases of the form 'the disposition to M (when S)', where 'M' and 'S' are references to a behaviour ('manifestation') and (optionally) some kind of influence of that behaviour ('stimulus'), respectively. Examples include the disposition to break when struck and the disposition to sing the Macarena.

We also count among dispositions so-called conventional (or 'covert') dispositions.[2] These include properties denoted by terms ending '-ility', '-ivity', '-icity', such as fragility, conductivity, and elasticity. Properties like these clearly have associated with them some manifestation and (arguably, in these cases) a stimulus. Consequently, we might say that, at least in paradigm cases, a fragile object (one which has the property of fragility) is disposed to break when struck, and an elastic object (one which has the property of elasticity) is disposed to return to a particular length after an applied load is released. We also include among conventional dispositions properties denoted by terms without the tell-tale suffix, such as courageousness, brittleness, and locquatiousness. Again, we can tell these are also dispositions by virtue of their inferential connection with a manifestation (and maybe a stimulus[3]).

---

[1] This is notable regardless of whether or not the pervasiveness of dispositions in science constitutes good reason to believe in powers (cf. Williams 2011).

[2] The terms 'canonical disposition' and 'conventional disposition' are originally from Choi (2003); see also Choi (2008). The terms 'overt' and 'covert' are from Bird (2007b).

[3] For detailed discussion of whether dispositions should be associated with stimulus and manifestation or just manifestation conditions see Vetter (2015, chs. 2 and 3).

Although we talk of dispositions as properties, we commit ourselves here only to a very 'light-touch' realism about them. In English, at least, we have the clauses '... is disposed to M', '... tends to M', etc., and also '... is fragile', '... is elastic'. We can also form nominalisations of these clauses: 'the disposition to M', 'the tendency to M', 'fragility', 'elasticity'. Under the fair assumption that sentences constructed with these nominalisations require a referent for the respective nominal, then all speakers commit themselves to the existence of dispositions when they honestly employ such terms. Nevertheless, we do not think the commitment forces any deep metaphysical position on speakers. In Bird's (2016, 2018) phrasing, we understand dispositions as 'predicatory' properties, to which we are 'ontologically uncommitted', imbuing them with 'no metaphysical baggage'. Predicatory properties are linguistic entities that feature in *truths* (propositions or sentences), whereas ontic entities are what make the truths true; dispositions can be understood in the former sense. That is, we want to remain uncommitted over whether dispositional properties are ontic, or whether talk of such properties is just a *façon de parler*, not to be taken literally but rather as a convenient shorthand when what is really intended by the expression is the corresponding dispositional predication of an object, where, in classical logic at least, predicates do not carry existential commitment (see, e.g., Quine 1948). In this way we hope that talk of dispositional (predicatory) properties will be fairly uncontroversial.

As we have seen, dispositions are necessarily tied up in some way with a specific manifestation and (according to some) a stimulus for that manifestation. More specifically, we take it that the necessary connection is a conceptual one, in the sense that mastery of dispositional terms demands knowledge of the way in which dispositions are tied up with their specific manifestation (and stimulus). At the very least, we take this to include knowledge of what the associated manifestation of the disposition is, but we think it also requires a more general comprehension of how and when manifestation is likely to occur. Section 2 is all about trying to spell out what this dispositional behaviour is and whether it can be specified in such a way as to provide an analysis of dispositions, i.e., conceptually revealing necessary and sufficient conditions for when a disposition is possessed by an object.

Powers are also necessarily tied up with the possibility for manifestation (perhaps given a stimulus), but in a different way than dispositions. Powers, as we employ the notion, are hypothesised properties that metaphysically explain the manifestation behaviour witnessed in disposed objects. Hence, powers are posited as the (ontic) truthmakers for true disposition *predications*. We follow others in referring to powers as a kind of 'causal basis' for dispositions, to be contrasted with other potential causal bases, like regularities among categorical properties. The point of saying this is not to suggest that the possession of powers causes the possession of dispositions, but rather that dispositional behaviour is (broadly speaking) causal behaviour, and, moreover, causal behaviour that warrants some metaphysical grounds. Powers' connection with manifestation behaviour is, therefore, a necessity to be established either through extended metaphysical or a posteriori reasoning.

There is a long-standing complaint with dispositions that their explanatory worth is limited. We can explain why the patient got sleepy by saying that the medicine they took is soporific. But it would be of little explanatory import to explain why the medicine makes those who ingest it feel drowsy by reference to it having the property of soporificity. After all, soporificity just is that dispositional property conceptually explicated in terms of the manifestation of drowsiness (after ingestion).[4] This suggests that the reason why ingesting the medicine induces drowsiness must make reference to something else. For example, we can say that the medicine is an opioid, meaning that it has certain empirically discoverable properties which are causally responsible for drowsiness. For some philosophers, these further empirically discoverable properties which individuate opioids may well be powers. If they are, they would be features of opioids which necessitate and explain the characteristics definitive of the dispositional behaviour witnessed by those who take them (note, that is not necessarily to say they necessitate drowsiness). Moreover, not only would these powers explain that behaviour, they would also explain why opioids are soporific, i.e., possess the disposition of soporificity.

It's the fact that powers are supposed to do this deeper explanatory work that makes them different in kind from dispositions. Unlike dispositions, powers (if they exist at all) are '*ontic*' properties. They are the sort of thing that populates the world, are metaphysically committing, and, for that reason, controversial. Section 3 discusses some of the central reasons philosophers have thought the commitment worth making alongside their explanation of dispositional behaviour, as well as some of the nuances behind how it is exactly that powers are necessarily and explanatorily related with dispositional behaviour.

The example of opioids and soporificity reveals a functionalist way of understanding the relationship between powers (if there are any) and dispositions which we think can be illuminating. According to this idea, dispositions are properties picked out by a causal role and powers (if they exist) are the realisers of those roles. So, for example, soporificity would be picked out by the causal process resulting in drowsiness. And if the reason opioids make one drowsy when

---

[4] For more on the discussion of dispositions' explanatory value, see Mumford (1998, 133–141).

ingested is that they possess certain powers necessarily and are explanatorily connected with the causal process of bringing about drowsiness, then these are the powers which realise the causal role implicated in opioids' soporificity.

There is much still to debate over the details of this functional understanding. One important question is whether or not dispositions are to be identified (a posteriori) with their realisers, so that soporificity *just is* a power which necessitates sleepiness upon ingestion. Such a view would nicely explain why dispositions seem so hard to conceptually analyse because it would render dispositions themselves real, occurrent, constituents of our ontology and so not apt to be analysed *away*. It would also confer upon dispositions the very explanatory causal role of their realisers without succumbing to problems of overdetermination. On the other hand, it seems to us that there may be some prospect of analysing dispositions, even if this analysis is not reductive in the sense that it cannot do without appeal to certain modal notions (see Section 2). Moreover, we sympathise with Prior et al. (1982) who argue that dispositions can (at least in principle) be realised by more than one causal occupant (e.g., it's not just the properties of opioids that can make us sleepy!). This would seem to demand that dispositions be instead identified with the second-order property of having some or other causal base which can perform a particular causal role.

Despite the importance of these kinds of issue, we leave their further discussion to another occasion (though see Hawthorne and Manley 2005; Mumford 1998; Prior 1985; Tugby 2022a, sec. 3.6 and 3.7). From hereon we keep discussion of dispositions and powers (Section 3) fairly distinct. This is reflected in how we have divided up writing this Element: one of us (Toby Friend) drafted this introduction and the discussion on dispositions (Section 2) while the other (Samuel Kimpton-Nye) drafted the discussion on powers (Section 3).[5]

2 Dispositions

2.1 Introduction

This section seeks a plausible analysis for dispositions. This is provided, we take it, by the provision of a schematic bi-conditional in which the left-hand side (the 'analysandum') is replaced by the attribution of a disposition and the right-hand side (the 'analysans') is replaced by non-trivial conditions true of exactly those things that satisfy the attribution, and knowledge of which would suffice for mastery of the dispositional concept. We follow tradition in aiming for a *single, unified* form of analysans rather than a plurality correspondent with different kinds of dispositional property.

---

[5] Inevitably, our individual philosophical preferences are not totally aligned and this is reflected in the emphasis placed for and against various views discussed in the longer sections.

The history of analysis of dispositions has its source in Carnap (1936). Carnap wanted to show how dispositions (more correctly, *dispositional expressions*) could be interpreted free of what he saw as unempirical terminology, such as modal operators and subjunctives. Ideally, a disposition like *solubility* was to be analysed by a relationship between a test condition (*stimulus*) and a resultant behaviour (*manifestation*) expressed using the minimal resources of first-order quantified logic. As we'll remark on further in the next subsection, philosophers (including Carnap) were quick to point out the difficulties of doing so and nowadays it is generally acknowledged that analyses of dispositions – insofar as they are possible – must employ some modal terms (see Bird 2012; McKitrick 2018, ch. 2; Mumford 1998, ch. 3; Schrenk 2017, ch. 2 for more on the history). The question, then, is *which modal terms*, and *in what way* must they be employed?

We begin by describing three platitudes about dispositions that justify the infamous 'Simple Conditional Analysis' (SCA) as our initial foil. We then introduce the heuristic of structural equations modelling. In the three subsections which follow (2.2, 2.3, and 2.4), we then use this heuristic to present problem cases for the preceding strategy for analysis before presenting another strategy in response. We go through various iterations (nine problem cases and eight strategies) until subsection 2.5, in which we sketch our own strategy for analysis that makes explicit reference to structural equations.

2.1.1 Three Platitudes

We begin by voicing some platitudes and points of consensus about dispositions.

First platitude: a disposition towards M is a 'directedness towards' some kind of paradigmatic behaviour conceptually associated with the disposition (Martin 2007; Molnar 2003; Tugby 2013). The term 'manifestation' is widely used for this behaviour, even though the behaviour might not be directly observable to the senses. The crucial idea behind 'directedness' is that being disposed towards a manifestation M should not entail actually doing M. An object disposed to behave in way M may not ever behave in way M.[6]

Second platitude: a disposition's manifestation can be triggered under specific conditions. For example, the sonority of a bell is manifested under striking with a hard object; malleability is manifested under pressure, etc. The term 'stimulus' is widely used to reference these conditions. Many, however, prefer the term 'manifestation partner', which is more conducive to understanding manifestation as an effect both of the disposition and whatever further conditions are

---

[6] However, this aspect of the platitude has been brought into question (Friend 2021).

needed (Heil 2010; Martin 2007; Mumford and Anjum 2011). Moreover, calling one property the 'stimulus' and the other the 'disposition' can often seem arbitrary, e.g., with the manifestation of heat exchange between a hot and a cold object. Nevertheless, 'manifestation partner' may go too far the other way, prohibiting any understanding of what triggers a manifestation being other than another property. Triggers could potentially be totality facts, absences, or background conditions.[7] Importantly, we won't assume that every disposition has a specific stimulus (see subsection 2.3.3, *Problem #6*). Some dispositions can be stimulated under a variety of conditions (e.g., breakability), other dispositions appear to have no stimulus requirements at all (e.g., loquacious-ness). A successful analysis should accommodate all these sorts of disposition.

Third platitude: the directedness of disposed objects towards manifestation is modal. We've remarked on the widely appreciated failure of excising modality from dispositional expressions' interpretation. The problem is that the dependence of manifestation on a stimulus seems obviously *conditional*. Yet the (non-modal) material conditional that manifestation occurs *if* the object is stimulated is satisfied by anything that is never stimulated (Carnap 1936). So, if dispositions were analysed by this conditional, an iron pot which never undergoes any applied stress would be falsely deemed just as fragile as a delicate porcelain vase. Instead, as many have remarked, what is needed is to link the stimulus and manifestation by a *counterfactual conditional*: manifestation *would occur were* the object stimulated. Counterfactual conditionals don't give rise to the same issue, since even if an object is never stimulated it typically *could be*.

Prior (1985, 5) called the connection between counterfactual conditionals and dispositions 'pre-theoretic common ground'; earlier, Quine (1974, 9) admitted (alongside Ryle 1949 and Storer 1951) that 'there is no denying that in its bumbling way, this intensional conditional somehow conveys the force of the dispositional idiom'; and later, Mumford (1998, 87) concurred with Martin (1994) that dispositions must be connected 'somehow' with conditionals. These remarks suggest that we could take the employment of counterfactual conditional analysans as a further platitude of dispositions. But there are prominent dissenting voices. Some eschew any attempt to characterise the modality of dispositionality in non–sui generis terms (Anjum and Mumford 2018; Martin 1994; Mumford and Anjum 2011). But even assuming these philosophers are wrong, others maintain that the dispositions' modal character is one of the *possibility* of manifestation rather than

---

[7] The term 'stimulus' also suggests that the associated conditions for manifestation must be *causes* of it. We think this is often a fair assumption (Handfield 2010; McKitrick 2010). Nevertheless, some dispositions may not be so easily thought of in this way, such as those in quantum mechanical contexts or Lagrangian mechanics (Katzav 2004; Nolan 2015; Smart and Thébault 2015). Space precludes us from engaging further with these cases.

manifestation's dependence on stimulus (Aimar 2019; Vetter 2015). We will explore these alternatives in subsections 2.3 and 2.4. Nevertheless, whichever option we pursue, the modality of dispositions' directedness is no longer in doubt.

With these platitudes in mind, we can now give a more precise description of what an analysis of dispositions must involve: it must spell out the 'directedness' platitude in terms of the modal implication of any disposed object's manifestation, including saying how, if at all, stimuli are involved. To that end we commence our search as many others have previously, by scrutinising the 'Simple Conditional Analysis' (where '$\square\rightarrow$' is the counterfactual conditional).

SCA. For all x, Dx if and only if $Sx \square\rightarrow Mx$.

Our go-to example, again unoriginal, is the analysis of *fragility*. Fragility is a disposition directed towards breaking, which we assume for the time being has the stimulus of (relatively low) applied stress. In the form of SCA, the analysis of fragility looks as follows:

FRAGILE. For all x, x is fragile if and only if were x to undergo (relatively low) stress x would break.

SCA (or properly speaking, its instances) is plagued by well-known counter-examples. We will go through the nine we have identified in the literature and discuss various strategies for avoiding them. However, before diving into the problem cases we introduce a heuristic for representation that we will make considerable use of this throughout this Element.

2.1.2 A Tool for Representation

Our demonstration of many of the problem cases will be atypical in that we make use of structural equations modelling. This might make us seem guilty of using a sledgehammer to crack a nut, since the formalism is rather more involved than anything employed in the current debate. Nevertheless, we ask the reader to persevere for two reasons. First, we think that once understood, structural equations models provide one of the clearest resources for identifying the nuances of each problem case. Second, structural equations will be of central importance to developing our novel strategy for analysis provided in subsection 2.5, and a familiarity with them will greatly facilitate its introduction.

A structural equation has the form $B(x) \Leftarrow f(A_1(x), \ldots, A_n(x))$ and expresses an asymmetric relationship of *numerical counterfactual dependency* of the left-hand variable property B of an object x on some function f of right-hand variable properties $A_1, \ldots, A_n$ of x (for conciseness we often omit the object variable). A structural equation therefore encodes lots of counterfactual information about how x would behave. Indeed, structural equations provide a counterfactual for every combination of values assigned to the right-hand variables (within some permitted range): if it *were* that $A_1(x) = a_1, \ldots, A_n(x) = a_n$ (i.e., each variable on the right-hand side were to take some specific distribution of determinate values) then *it would be that* $B(x) = f(a_1, \ldots, a_n) = b$.

Structural equations are bread and butter for contemporary causal analysis in science and philosophy of causation (Pearl 2000; Hitchcock 2001; Woodward 2003; Halpern and Pearl 2005). Causal results and hypotheses are typically expressed in terms of structural equations *models* (SEMs), an ordered pair (V, E) of variable set V and structural equations set E such that every variable in V is either on the left-hand side of at most one equation in E (and so dependent on other variables in V) or else is 'exogenous' (having its value determined by factors outside of the model). Associated with any SEM is a causal graph where the variables in V are nodes and directed edges (arrows) lead from one variable A to another B just in case A features in the right-hand side of a structural equation in which B is the left-hand variable.

Our aim is to use SEMs to describe the causal relationships relevant to dispositional behaviour. These models will therefore include 'stimulus variables', 'manifestation variables', and 'disposition variables', which take values ranging over whether (and to what degree) an object is stimulated, manifests, and has some disposition, respectively.

Let's consider the SEM involving a fragile object x described in Table 1.

Table 1 displays the model's variables ($FR(x), ST(x)$ and $BR(x)$) and how to interpret their possible values. For example, if the variable $FR(x) = 1$ this indicates that x is fragile, and if $FR(x) = 0, x$ is *not* fragile. Table 1 also displays whether the variables have a structural equation or not. In this model, only one variable is not exogenous $(BR(x))$ and so is the only variable with a structural equation $(BR(x) \Leftarrow FR(x) \times ST(x))$. The model's equation tells us that the values of $BR(x)$ are determined by $FR(x) \times ST(x)$. Moreover, it tells us that the determination is robust under counterfactual variations of the right-hand variable's values: for any combination of values for $FR(x)$ and $ST(x)$, if those variables were to take those values, $BR(x)$ would take the value given by the equation.

Since the one structural equation for the present model reveals $BR(x)$'s dependence on $FR(x)$ and $ST(x)$, the causal graph for this model will have two directed edges indicating causal influence of $FR(x)$ and $ST(x)$ on $BR(x)$, as displayed in Figure 1.

If we take this SEM to characterise causal relationships any object x whatsoever can be involved in, then it predicts FRAGILE. For it entails that if x were fragile $(FR(x) = 1)$ and were stimulated $(ST(x) = 1)$ then it would break $(BR(x) = FR(x) \times ST(x) = 1)$, whereas if x were not fragile

Table 1 Details for a causal model for fragility

Variables			
Symbol	Possible values	Interpretation	Structural equations
FR	1	x is fragile	(Exogenous)
	0	x is not fragile	
ST	1	x undergoes stress	(Exogenous)
	0	x does not undergo stress	
BR	1	x breaks	$BR \Leftarrow FR \times ST$
	0	x does not break	

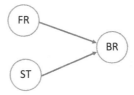

Figure 1 Causal graph for a simple causal model for fragility

$(FR(x) = 0)$ and were stimulated $(ST(x) = 1)$ then it would not break $(BR(x) = FR(x) \times ST(x) = 0)$. Assuming possible worlds are strongly centred on the actual world (so that the actual world is the closest possible world in which any true proposition is true) then FRAGILE is entailed. However, the SEM predicts further counterfactuals not directly relevant to the truth of FRAGILE. For instance, it predicts that if something were fragile $(FR(x) = 1)$ but did not undergo stress $(ST(x) = 0)$ then it wouldn't break $(BR(x) = FR(x) \times ST(x) = 0)$. Although this kind of counterfactual is not part of traditional dispositions' analyses, we take it to be plausible in many contexts. In subsection 2.5 we will argue that, in fact, it should be a feature of fragility's analysis.

Given how widely dispositions are thought to be causally implicating we find it surprising that SEMs are yet to be invoked in discussion of their analysis. As we aim to show, SEMs provide a fertile heuristic for displaying many of dispositions' causal features. But it's important not to get carried away. Structural equations models do not add any metaphysical assumptions about the relationships among those included variables than are already implied by the counterfactuals encoded in their equations. Instead, SEMs' value comes from the fact they encode far more counterfactual information than is available from any single conditional. It is this feature which makes them instrumental for describing problem cases, and also for providing the basis of a new strategy for analysis (see Section 2.5).

2.2 One-Conditional Analyses

Here we look at four problems which have brought SCA into question, and at strategies for response which keep within the constraints of a one-conditional analysis, i.e., analyses that employ a single counterfactual conditional in the analysans.

2.2.1 Problem #1: Masks

The disposition of an appropriately stimulated object is 'masked' when it fails to manifest due to interference.[8] A classic example is when a fragile vase fails to break when subject to stress because it is packed in bubble wrap (Johnston 1992). Another example is when an antidote is taken to counteract the disposition of ingested poison to cause harm (Bird 1998). This kind of causal interference is easily captured in an SEM, as described in Table 2. The associated causal graph is displayed in Figure 2.

The counterfactuals entailed by this SEM are more complex than instances of SCA allow. A typical SCA for *poisonousness* might be the following:

For all x, x is poisonous if and only if were x ingested harm would occur.

Table 2 Details for a causal model for masking poisonousness

Variables			
Symbol	**Possible values**	**Interpretation**	**Structural equations**
P	1	x is poisonous	(Exogenous)
	0	x is not poisonous	
I	1	x is ingested by agent	(Exogenous)
	0	x is not ingested by agent	
A	1	x is accompanied by antidote	(Exogenous)
	0	x is not accompanied by antidote	
H	1	Agent comes to harm	$H \Leftarrow (P \times I) \times (1 - A)$
	0	Agent does not come to harm	

---

[8] We do not here distinguish masks from 'antidotes' (or 'interferers'), where the latter but not the former act after the stimulus has taken place (cf. Paoletti 2021).

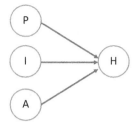

Figure 2 Causal graph for masking poisonousness

But this is not true in the above SEM since it is consistent with the model that x is poisonous ($P = 1$) and yet harm doesn't occur ($H = 0$) because the antidote is ingested ($A = 1$). Masks therefore present a counterexample to the analysans in SCAs being a necessary condition for dispositions, since something can have a disposition but, due to the presence of a mask, fail to obey the associated counterfactual.

2.2.2 Problem #2: Alterers

Dispositions are subject to 'altering' when the stimulus of a disposition influences whether (and to what degree) an object has that disposition. This can happen in two ways: either an object is caused to lose a disposition when stimulus occurs, as when a live wire with the disposition to conduct electricity is caused to go dead when touched because of the presence of a fuse; or an object is caused to gain a disposition when stimulus occurs, as when a dead wire has a sensor (an 'electro-fink') which causes it to become live when touched. Charlie Martin (1994) is credited with being the first to discuss these kinds of case and used the terms 'reverse-cycle fink' and 'fink', respectively. We employ Johnston's (1992, 232–3) more general 'altering', since the stimulus in either case *alters* the dispositional status of the object.

Consider the SEM described in Table 3. The associated causal graph is displayed in Figure 3. What the graph clearly shows is that, in cases of altering, there is more than one effect being considered. Not only is whether x manifests (C) an effect of whether x has the disposition (L) and is stimulated (T), but whether x has the disposition is also an effect of whether x is stimulated.

As with masking, the true counterfactuals of this SEM are more complex than those in instances of SCA. A typical SCA for *being live* is the following (cf. Martin 1994):

> For all x, x is live if and only if were x touched by a conductor current would flow from x to the conductor.

Table 3 Details for a causal model of altering being electrically live

Variables			
Symbol	**Possible values**	**Interpretation**	**Structural equations**
T	1	x is touched by a conductor	(Exogenous)
	0	x is not touched by a conductor	
L	1	x is live	$L \Leftarrow 1 - T$
	0	x is not live	
C	1	Current flows from x to the conductor	$C \Leftarrow L \times T$
	0	Current does not flow from x to the conductor	

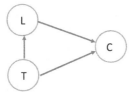

Figure 3 Causal graph for altering being electrically live

But this is not true in the foregoing SEM, since if the x were touched by a conductor $(T = 1)$ then x would no longer be live $(L = 1 - T = 0)$, and so current would not flow from x to the conductor $(C = L \times T = 0)$. The above case of altering therefore presents a counterexample to the necessity of the analysans in SCAs, since something can have a disposition, but due to the presence of a stimulus which removes the disposition, the disposed object fails to obey the associated counterfactual. To model the other altering case where stimulus confers the disposition upon the object, we need only revise the structural equation for L from $L \Leftarrow (1 - T)$ to $L \Leftarrow T$ (the graph stays the same). This would then present a counterexample to the *sufficiency* of the analysans in SCAs, since x would satisfy the associated counterfactual while failing to have the disposition.

2.2.3 Problem #3: Mimickers

A disposition is mimicked by objects without that disposition but behave as though they do. Styrofoam plates are not fragile. If a plate undergoes an applied stress, it makes a distinctive sound that, when in earshot, provokes the hater of Styrofoam to tear it up. So, in such circumstances the plate would break were it stressed (the example is in Lewis 1997, attributed to Daniel Nolan).

Consider the SEM described in Table 4. The associated causal graph is displayed in Figure 4.

Table 4 Details for a causal model for mimicking fragility

Variables			
Symbol	Possible values	Interpretation	Structural equations
FR	1	x is fragile	(Exogenous)
	0	x is not fragile	
ST	1	x undergoes stress	(Exogenous)
	0	x does not undergo stress	
E	1	x is within earshot of a hater of Styrofoam	(Exogenous)
	0	x is not within earshot of a hater of Styrofoam	
H	1	A hater of Styrofoam overhears x being stressed	$H \Leftarrow E \times ST$
	0	A hater of Styrofoam doesn't overhear x being stressed	
BR	1	x breaks	$BR \Leftarrow (FR + H - FR \times H) \times ST$
	0	x does not break	

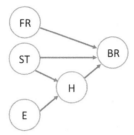

Figure 4 Causal graph for mimicking fragility

The true counterfactuals of this SEM are more complex than SCA allows. Our earlier SCA for fragility (FRAGILE) entailed that the following is true for any *x*.

Only if *x* is fragile then were *x* to undergo stress it would break.

But this is not true in the above SEM, since it is consistent with the model that *x* undergoes stress ($ST = 1$) and breaks ($BR = 1$) yet fails to be fragile ($FR = 0$), so long as the hater of Styrofoam is within earshot ($E = 1$). Mimickers therefore present a counterexample to the sufficiency of the analysans in SCAs, since the associated counterfactual can be true while *x* fails to have the corresponding disposition.

2.2.4 Problem #4: Tricks

Tricks are discussed by Contessa (2016). Like mimickers, tricks also look like displays of dispositionality when they are not. Contessa's example involves a mug of coffee cooling down. It is not, Contessa maintains, disposed to cool down when someone says 'Abracadabra' over it. Nevertheless, it would cool down were someone to do so, since it is destined to cool down anyway due to the immutable laws of thermodynamics (perhaps we should grant it has the disposition to cool, simpliciter). As with mimickers, the dispositional behaviour seems to be a trick, a merely circumstantial satisfaction of the counterfactual relationship between stimulus and manifestation. Unlike mimickers, however, the possibility of manifestation is independent of whether the object is stimulated; the object is destined to manifest anyway.

Let's work through another 'tricky' case. A non-fragile mug will be crushed in a hydraulic press. Therefore, if the mug were to undergo (relatively low) stress it would break.[9] Consider the model described in Table 5. The associated causal graph is displayed in Figure 5.

---

[9] As one reviewer pointed out, there seems to be a difference between our example and Contessa's. Plausibly, the mug has the disposition to cool (simpliciter) despite not having the disposition to cool when someone says 'Abracadabra' over it. By contrast, the mug plausibly *does not* have the

Table 5 Details for a causal model for fragility tricks

Variables

Symbol	Possible values	Interpretation	Structural equations
FR	1	x is fragile	(Exogenous)
	0	x is not fragile	
ST	1	x undergoes stress	(Exogenous)
	0	x does not undergo stress	
CR	1	x is crushed in a hydraulic press	(Exogenous)
	0	x is not crushed in a hydraulic press	
BR	1	x breaks	$BR \Leftarrow (FR \times ST + CR) - (FR \times ST \times CR)$
	0	x does not break	

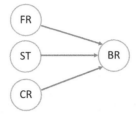

Figure 5 Causal graph for fragility tricks

The true counterfactuals of this SEM are more complex than SCA would seem to allow. Our earlier SCA for fragility entailed the following for any x:

> Only if x is fragile, then were x to undergo stress it would break.

But this is not true for cases described by the SEM, since it is consistent with the model that x undergoes stress ($ST = 1$) and breaks ($BR = 1$) and yet fails to be fragile ($FR = 0$), because it will be crushed by a hydraulic press ($C = 1$). Tricks therefore present a counterexample to the sufficiency of the analysans in SCA, since something can obey the associated counterfactual, but due to the tricky circumstances, fail to have the corresponding disposition.

2.2.5 Strategy A: Getting Specific

We now turn to consider strategies for responding to problem cases #1–#4. The problem cases capitalise on the assumption that the antecedent of the characterising conditionals in instances of SCA only refer to a single influence. For instance, in the case of FRAGILE the antecedent is 'x undergoes (relatively low) applied stress'. Consequently, the antecedent is satisfied even when x is wrapped in bubble wrap, is subject to altering, is about to be crushed in a hydraulic press, is within earshot of the hater of Styrofoam, etc. But what if the antecedent of the analysing conditional included additional qualifications that these further conditions do not hold? More generally, what if we avoid the problem cases by *getting more specific* in the conditional's antecedent?

The issue with this strategy is that there is potentially an infinity of relevant factors which must be accounted for. Just focus on the specifications required to

---

disposition to break, let alone the disposition to break under relatively low applied stress (as per fragile objects). We think the apparent difference could be challenged (see subsection 2.2.6, *Strategy B: Denial*). But either way, both examples are 'tricky' in the sense that they behave as though they have a particular disposition because they are destined to behave that way anyway. Hence, both can be modelled by structurally identical models.

avoid counterexamples to FRAGILITY due to masks. A fragile vase can be protected from breaking when under applied stress not just by bubble wrap, but also by changing the material of the striking object, by striking it in a vat of honey, by striking it incredibly slowly, or any of the numerous ways of reducing the force of the striking object; and of course there's always the possibility – the philosopher's favourite – that a nearby wizard casts a spell which protects the vase in some way unknown to physics. Presumably, the options for alters, tricks, and mimickers are similarly profuse.

Whatever antecedent goes into the characterising conditional of a disposition will have to be enormously complex, if not open-ended, if it is to cover every possible eventuality explicitly (Manley and Wasserman 2008 and Anjum and Mumford 2018). Perhaps some added complexity could be tolerated, but it is surely implausible that the analysans has the level of complexity it would have to have to accommodate all the potential eventualities of the sort described above. Given the ease with which we conceptually grasp dispositions like *fragility*, it cannot be that we learn anything remotely like that. Of course, if our task was other than *analysis*, we might be willing to put up with an element of open-endedness. Analysis requires that we give conceptually graspable necessary and sufficient conditions for the presence of a disposition; an open-ended list of conditions can't do that. Consequently, the *Getting Specific* strategy should be rejected.

2.2.6 Strategy B: Denial

Here is a different strategy. Problems #1–#4 rest on intuitions about whether the presence of interfering factors influences whether something has a disposition. The presence of a mask doesn't – so the intuitions go – stop a thing having the disposition it has, it only *masks* it. By contrast, the presence of an altering stimulus does change whether something has a disposition. If mimickers and tricks are to be a problem, intuition must have it that the presence of a mimicker or trick doesn't confer a disposition on a thing, it only 'mimics' it. One strategy is, therefore, to *deny* these intuitions.

Choi has denied the intuition in the case of mimickers. 'Contrary to appearances, [SCA] is not troubled with the case of the Styrofoam dish. . . . [I]t does not pose any threat . . . because [the dish] indeed has the disposition to break in response to being struck' (Choi 2005, 182–3).[10] He has also denied it in the case of masks.

> [I]f an object is situated in a stimulating circumstance c but does not exhibit
> a manifestation m because of the masking operation of a dispositional antidote
> [mask], we will deny that it has the disposition to exhibit m in response to being

---

[10] Choi is in fact defending Lewis's *revised* conditional analysis not SCA (see subsection 2.2.7), but the point carries over.

situated in c; instead we will ascribe to it the disposition to exhibit m in response
to being situated in c in the absence of the antidote. (Choi 2008, 797–8)

Choi doesn't give an argument for these claims except to say that opposition
to them is poorly justified. Hájek makes a similar remark about altering.

In the . . . wire case, the simple conditional analysis would have us judge that
[the wire is disposed at noon to conduct electrical current when touched by
a conductor] is true. And so do I. The wire is disposed at noon to conduct
electrical current when touched by a conductor. After all, its intrinsic nature is
disposed to change when the electro-fink machine operates on it. And thanks
to its intrinsic nature changing, it is then disposed to conduct electrical
current; after all, it has changed into a live wire! (Hájek 2020, 4798)

Hájek justifies this by pointing out that altering stimuli can only interfere with
the dispositions of the object because that object is receptive to change, where
that receptiveness, Hájek suggests, must be a further disposition. Lastly,
although neither Choi nor Hájek consider it, the *Denial* strategy may also be
effective against tricks. Perhaps in the end it is correct to say that a mug of hot
coffee has the disposition to cool down when one says 'Abracadabra' over it.

Choi and Hájek admit that the strategy only works in general for 'canonical'
dispositions (see Section 1). Arguably, neither the presence of the hater of
Styrofoam, bubble wrap, nor the hydraulic press provide a counterexample to
SCA's analysis of the disposition to break when stressed; nor does the presence of
an electro-fink provide a counterexample to SCA's analysis of the disposition to
conduct electricity when touched. But these circumstances *do* still provide
counterexamples to SCA's analysis of *fragility* and *being a live wire*, respectively.
The reason for this is that, unlike canonical dispositions, the dispositions of
fragility and *being a live wire* are intrinsic, which is to say, roughly, that whether
an object has them or not is independent of whatever is going on beyond them.
Given that conventional dispositions are often those we are most interested in
(Hájek 2020; Vetter 2015), and many conventional dispositions seem to be
intrinsic, this puts a severe limitation on the *Denial* strategy.

Even granting the restriction to canonical dispositions, there are reasons to
query whether the *Denial* strategy always works. Choi claims that a vase wrapped
in bubble wrap is not disposed to break when stressed but is *disposed to break
when stressed in the absence of the bubble wrap*. Should we say the same for
a vase *not* wrapped in bubble wrap? If we do, then we descend a slippery slope,
having to deny that any vase is disposed to break when stressed, or indeed even
when stressed in the absence of bubble wrap, since it could be wrapped in
Styrofoam instead, or have the protection of a wizard, etc. As we've seen already,
we shouldn't allow dispositions to have such complex analysans. If, however, the

dispositions of otherwise identical wrapped and unwrapped vases are different, we'll have to deny that *any* disposition is intrinsic, since even the dispositions an unprotected vase has will be dependent on the *absence* of extrinsic protection. We might grant that some dispositions are extrinsic, but it is less plausible that dispositions are inevitably extrinsic in this sense.[11] Worse still, since the context every vase is in is slightly different, we'd have to claim that the maskable dispositions of each vase are unique. This seems to us absurd. On reflection, it appears more reasonable to say of both wrapped and unwrapped (but otherwise identical) vases that they share the disposition to break when stressed, contrary to Choi's *Denial* strategy for the problem of masks.[12]

2.2.7 Strategy C: So Long As

Another strategy for dealing with problems #1–#4 is to find some way to characterise dispositions as manifesting given the stimulus only *so long as* further influences are absent.

An early example of this kind of approach is Lewis's (1997) 'Revised Conditional Analysis' (RCA).

> RCA. Something x has disposition D at time t iff, for some intrinsic property B that x has at t and for some time t' after t, if x were to undergo stimulus S at time t and so long as it retains property B until time t', S and x's having of B would jointly be an x-complete cause[13] of x's giving response M.[14] (Lewis 1997, 157)

The motivation behind RCA was to avoid the problem of alterers, for which, Lewis assumed, the relevant intrinsic properties of an object change under stimulus. We won't elaborate here on why it fails to avoid all the other problem cases (see Bird 2007b, 27–36; Martin 2007, 19–21). Moreover, its solution to the problem of alters is uniquely problematic, since it requires that the disposition must be retained

---

[11] For all we say in this section, Hájek may be right that there is always some residual extrinsic dependence on the laws or the environment.

[12] We are also suspicious of the strategy's employment in the case of alterers. Hájek claims that a wire hooked up to an electro-fink is disposed to conduct when touched, since it is disposed to be made live by the electro-fink when touched and live wires are disposed (absent further altering) to conduct when touched. But how far should we go with this reasoning? Is a pencil disposed to get sharper when the wind blows if it's placed in the right sequence of convoluted contraptions? More generally, is anything which Ms also disposed to M when the big bang occurs? These further commitments seem to be implied by Hájek's reasoning and yet are too absurd to be endorsed. Bird (2007b, 32–3) offers a similar criticism of the *Denial* strategy for reverse-cycle finks.

[13] As Bird (2007b, 27) summarises, 'An x-complete cause of y includes all the intrinsic properties of x which causally contribute to y's occurrence. This stipulation is required to rule out certain other finkish counterexamples.'

[14] Lewis originally phrased RCA in terms of canonical dispositions. But we don't see why it must be so constrained.

for some time after stimulus in non-altering cases. But, plausibly, an applied stress can cause something fragile to break instantaneously (as soon as the stress induces acceleration), and once broken, something (often, at least) can't be broken again.[15] Hence, its fragility will not be retained for any time upon stimulus.

A more flat-footed *So Long As* strategy introduces into analysis the qualification that the antecedent conditions lead to manifestation so long as masks, alterers, mimckers, and tricks are absent (cf. Bird 2007b, 59–60). Another comes from Hüttemann (2004), who proposes that the analysing counterfactual holds so long as the disposed object is *in isolation*. Vaguer and potentially more inclusive qualifications have also been proposed, e.g., that the manifestation occurs 'in normal circumstances', in 'ordinary circumstances', or 'ceteris paribus' (Bird 1998; Choi 2008; Cross 2005; Kistler 2020; Martin 1994; Mumford 1998; Steinberg 2010). We count all of these cases as instances of the *So Long As* strategy.

Some of these suggestions appear liable to circularity. For example, employing the concepts of *mask* and *alterer* in analyses would give rise to circularities if their own definitions can't be given without reference to dispositions (as we might expect). And what could 'normal' circumstances be if not those in which the manifestation occurs given the stimulus? Choi (2008) defends a non-circular understanding of 'ordinary', but this arguably leaves too much down to the minds of 'those who possess the corresponding dispositional concept'. Moreover, both qualifications of normalcy and ordinariness appear susceptible to Fara's (2005) complaint that something can normally/ordinarily *M* if it is *S* just because circumstances make the manifestation anyway likely (such circumstances would be like generalised tricks). Finally, the notion of isolation is also fraught with interpretational issues – isolation from what: properties, objects? And what is isolation? Presumably not independence from accompaniment, since some dispositions will only manifest in a suitably populated environment (e.g., containing quantum fields, a breathable atmosphere, etc.).

A more carefully presented instance of the *So Long As* strategy comes from Contessa (2013), who gives an account of how to understand masks and alterers in terms of 'destructive interference' and mimickers in terms of 'constructive interference' so that there is no circularity or vacuity in qualifying the conditional dependence of manifestation on stimulus *so long as nothing interferes*.[16] Crucial to the

---

[15] In some sense, the stimulus (applied stress) does 'alter' the disposition, yet we take it that this doesn't count as a case of altering in the sense above, since breaking is the manifestation of fragility.

[16] Contessa appears to take finks and reverse-cycle finks to be forms of destructive interference. We suspect, however, that finks count as constructive interference. But these details don't influence the overall success of Contessa's analysis.

analysis is the contrast between intrinsic and extrinsic dispositions, and Contessa seeks to define the latter in terms of the former. Part of the purpose behind this is to provide a principled distinction between mimickers and extrinsic dispositions. Roughly, only genuine extrinsic dispositions (and not mimickers) are such that there is some further intrinsic disposition of the disposed object whose stimulus–manifestation dependency contributes to the observed behaviour. According to Contessa, mimickers do not 'piggyback' on intrinsic dispositions in this way.

Contessa's distinction between extrinsic dispositions and mimickers seems to us problematic. Surely the disposition of the Styrofoam plate to make a particular sound when stressed contributes to the fact that it breaks when the hater of Styrofoam is in earshot. The plate's disposition to break when stressed therefore piggybacks on some intrinsic dispositions. But we do not want to say the plate is fragile. Indeed, it is a paradigm case of mimicking. Even without considering further problem cases, therefore, Contessa's approach to responding to problems #1–#4 may not be the final story for analysis of dispositions. And he admits that it does not respond to the problem of tricks (Contessa 2016, 590 fn. 5). In sum, we have yet to find a convincing account among *So Long As* strategies, or one-conditional approaches more generally.

2.3 No-Conditionals Analyses

Here, we engage with additional problems for dispositions' analysis which, in addition to the foregoing, have motivated philosophers to abandon the use of conditionals altogether.

2.3.1 Problem #5: Chancy Dispositions

Hájek (2020, 4801) points out that if one wishes to undermine conditional analyses of dispositions then 'finkish [i.e., altering] cases are needlessly baroque'. That's because the associated counterfactuals are often falsified in much more ordinary ways. His key examples are chancy dispositions.[17] An object might be disposed to behave in way X if subject to Y and yet not be such that were it subjected to Y then it would behave in way X, since there is only a high but non-maximal probability of it behaving in way X if subjected to Y. For instance, an object with such a disposition might be *actually* subjected to Y and not behave in way X, thereby falsifying the disposition's associated counterfactual (assuming strong centring). Likewise, an object may *not* be disposed to behave in way X if subject to Y yet be such that were it subjected to Y then it

---

[17] Hájek also offers another example: 'unspecificity of the stimulus' (not to be confused with our *Problem #6: Unspecific Stimuli*, subsection 2.3.3). We take this issue to be covered implicitly in discussion of Problem #7 (subsection 2.3.4).

would X, since there is only a probability <1 of it not behaving in way X if subjected to Y. For instance, an object without such a disposition might be actually subjected to Y and behave in way X, thereby satisfying the disposition's associated conditional. Chancy dispositions therefore present problems both for the necessity and sufficiency of the analysans in instances of SCA.[18]

Tempting as it may be, it's no use responding to the threat of chancy dispositions by claiming that the world is in fact deterministic, or is deterministic for all intents and purposes at the macroscopic level. Under standard 'collapse' interpretations of quantum mechanics, a disposition to radioactively decay or quantum tunnel through some material might be *fundamentally chancy*. And such indeterminacies could, for all we know, 'percolate up to macroscopic objects' (Hájek 2020, 4804); see also Hawthorne 2005). Hence, Hájek (2020, 4804) notes that 'fragility is as paradigmatic a case of a disposition as there can be – it is by far the most common example in the literature – and yet given its sensitivity to facts about molecular bonding, it is surely not sure-fire (even when it is nearly so)'. Likewise, objects may fail to be fragile even if, given the sensitivity to facts about molecular bonding, it is not certain that it won't break under relatively low applied stress. These kinds of chanciness have been variously referred to as '(reverse) Achilles heels' (Manley and Wasserman 2008; Vetter 2015) or 'weak/strong spots' (Aimar 2019; Hájek 2020), since they are often due to a part of the disposed/undisposed object which is uncharacteristically undisposed/disposed to behave in the relevant way.[19]

2.3.2 Strategy D: Generics

A strategy for response to chancy dispositions, which would also address problems #1–#4, would be to substitute the conditional in SCA with a generic:

GENERIC. For all *x*, D*x* if and only if *x* M's (when S'd).

The generic in GENERIC is like a conditional, but instead of entailing that *x* would M if it were subject to S (on some occasion), the statement makes a generalisation over all the occasions where it is subject to S and, crucially, in a way that tolerates exceptions. This seems just what is needed to address

---

[18] Max Kistler has asked us what distinguishes an object disposed to X when Y from one which can X when Y by chance. We're not sure but suspect surpassing some contextually determined threshold of probability to X given Y may suffice.

[19] We needn't suppose that indeterminacy can only owe its provenance to the quantum domain. Arguably, materially closed systems are disposed to increase in entropy over time irrespective of the status of quantum determinacy. The overwhelming majority of such systems will do so, but given enough instances some small proportion will not. Crucially, that's not because of external contextual factors nor is it clearly due to quantum indeterminacy, but because the microdynamics conspire in an improbable way to minimise or maintain a stable entropy instead.

chancy dispositions as well as masks and alterers. Moreover, a generic is not assertible about an object given merely that there is some instance of it being S'd which M's. There must be reason to expect that it will *in general* M when S'd. This suggests that GENERIC may have the means to respond to problems of mimickers and tricks too.

There are nevertheless many issues facing this *Generics* strategy. One hurdle is to avoid the issue (noted in subsection 2.2 above with qualifications of normalcy) that it can be true of some objects that they (generically/normally) manifest when stimulated purely because some independent circumstance makes manifestation likely. Fara's (2005) solution is to requrie that the disposed object Ms when S'd *in virtue of its intrinsic properties*. We know, however, that some dispositional behaviour is due to extrinsic facts (Mckitrick 2003). An object's weight gives it a disposition to produce a reading on weighing scales, but the weight is not fully intrinsic, since it is partly a consequence of the gravitational field it is in. Anyway, Fara's qualification may not even work for intrinsic dispositions. A machine programmed to print designs on non-fragile mugs might always fail (due to a software error) to print a paisley design properly when requested to. Consequently, the machine operators normally put the paisley-designed mugs in the incinerator rather than send them to Sales. In this case, paisley mugs break ultimately in virtue of an intrinsic property (their paisley design), and though they aren't fragile, they nevertheless break when stressed.

Another issue with GENERIC is that it seems to imply that any D has been or will be S'd. But there need be no such instances for the corresponding disposition. For example, if a bell is never struck, it seems wrong to say that it rings when struck, while it seems perfectly coherent to say that it is *disposed to* ring when struck (Wasserman 2011, 433–7).

A potential solution to both issues involves reference to kind-level generalisations. Lowe (2007, 107) endorses the idea that a disposition for something x to M when S'd can be understood in terms of x being a member of some kind K, where it is a law that Ks M when S. This is perfectly consistent with x itself never being S'd. The qualification that Ks M when S'd is a law also establishes an explanatory connection between M and S, thereby avoiding the problem of instances M-ing when S'd due to reasons independent of S (cf. the suggestion by Quine 1970 and discussed by Wasserman 2011, 437–9). However, Wasserman complains that since the kinds which feature in laws of nature must be natural kinds, Lowe's qualification will be too restrictive. It just seems false that all instances of any natural kind share the same dispositions (e.g., cats need not all be disposed to purr), nor does it seem reasonable to restrict disposed objects to instances of a natural kind.

2.3.3 Problem #6: Unspecific Stimuli

The *Generics* strategy also shares a problem with the one-conditional analyses so far discussed. Notice first that all these accounts require that dispositions must be conceptually associated with some or other stimulus. As we mentioned in subsection 2.1.1, however, this isn't always the case. Molnar (2003, 85–6) gives the example of the muon,[20] which has the disposition to spontaneously decay into an electron, a neutrino, and an antineutrino. Manley and Wasserman (2008) suggest that *loquaciousness* and *irascibility* are dispositions to manifest, respectively, talking and anger independently of whether or not they are provoked to do so (see also Fara 2005, 70). Hájek (2020) likewise suggests the disposition of a photon to follow a geodesic. It seems implausible that any of these dispositions is conceptually associated with a stimulus condition.

Fara (2005) has argued that generic analyses *can* deal with this problem of 'absent stimuli' simply by making the 'when S'd' clause optional. He tentatively suggests this is a further benefit of generics over conditionals. However, the problem of absent stimuli may not be all that bothersome for conditional approaches either. In the case of loquaciousness, for example, the fan of conditionals can claim that the relevant 'stimulus' is the trivial condition of anything whatsoever occurring, or the occurrence of some logical truth.[21]

Regardless, there remains a similar but more troublesome problem for both conditionals and generics accounts, not that there may be only vacuous stimulus requirements, but that the required stimuli may be *wholly unspecific*. For example, things are breakable if they can be caused to break (as opposed to breaking spontaneously). So breakability manifests under a stimulus, but one that is unspecific. This is troublesome since both one-conditional and generics strategies require that *if* a disposition needs stimulating in order to manifest then the stimulus should be specifiable, either in the antecedent of a counterfactual or as the 'restrictor' of a generic. In the case of breakability, what can we put in either place? An object is breakable if *something* can cause it to break. But the condition that the manifestation occurs when caused by something, or would occur were it caused by something, is trivially satisfied by everything. There doesn't seem a sensible analysis either view can provide.

---

[20] Molnar calls this spontaneity a power, but in the context of discussion of analysis; hence, we appropriate the example as a disposition.

[21] A different option draws on Lewis's RCA and analyses manifestations as caused by their disposition whether or not stimuli are relevant (Hauska 2015).

2.3.4 Problem #7: Disjunctive Multi-Track Dispositions

Another problem for both one-conditional and generics strategies is highlighted by Vetter (2015), and concerns dispositions whose instances don't all manifest in the same way. First notice that the following two conditions (or something very similar) are inevitable commitments under either strategy for analysis of any arbitrary disposition D:

1. Being such as to M were it S'd, or M-ing (when S'd), is necessary for having D.
2. Manifesting D can only be achieved by exhibiting M in response to S.

Condition 1 is entailed by analyses of the form SCA and GENERIC (variations can be given corresponding with the other one-conditional and generic strategies considered already). Condition 2 is not entailed by any analysis, but it is a natural presupposition. If D would count as manifesting by exhibiting some behaviour other than M, or by exhibiting M in some other way than in response to S, then any analysis of D should take that into account.

In combination these conditions lead to a dilemma. Take *fragility*, which we agreed to understand as manifesting under (relatively low) applied stress. Some fragile things will break under even the slightest stress, others require more, though still not as much as non-fragile objects. So let there be some threshold value T such that for any fragile object there is a minimum value $T' < T$ of stress that will break it. Now pick some object a which will break if subject to a stress of at least T'_a. It is not true of it that a will break for *any* applied stress less than T, since it only breaks if the applied stresses are T'_a or above. Hence the stimulus for fragility can't be the broad condition of any applied stress under T, since not every instance of such a stimulus on a fragile object will result in manifestation, contrary to condition 1. If, instead, we choose a more specific stimulus, say applied stresses above T'_a, then when other objects *do* break from applied stresses lower than T'_a this cannot count as a display of *fragility* on pain of contravening condition 2. But something breaking under even lower stresses than those which can count as a stimulus for fragility (e.g., T'_a) will surely also be a manifestation of fragility (context permitting).

The dilemma described here is one of *disjunctive multi-track dispositions*.[22] Not all of the ways in which a disposition like fragility can be made to manifest can make every instance of that disposition manifest. Hence, if fragility is to be

---

[22] The coinage is our own and is to be contrasted with what we later refer to as 'conjunctively multi-track dispositions' (see subsection 2.4.4, *Problem #9*). Nevertheless, the identification of both associated problems should be attributed to Vetter (2015). Our hope is to have made the distinction between problems clearer.

analysed in terms of an association (a 'track') between stimulus and manifest-ation it would have to be a disjunction of multiple such associations: fragility's instances can break under this stimulus or that or ... etc. Since no one-conditional or generics strategy entertains such a disjunction of stimulus–manifestation relationships, they cannot address this problem.

2.3.5 Strategy E: Possibilities

Some of the aforementioned problems have been the explicit motivation behind some abandoning a relational analysis of dispositions altogether. Instead of a relationship (e.g., conditional or generic) between stimulus and manifestation, these theorists hope to capture dispositions monadically, in terms of the *possibility for* manifestation (Aimar 2019; Vetter 2011, 2014, 2015). At its most simplistic, the schema for such analyses is as follows:

POSSIBILITY. For all x, D x if and only if x can M.

The schema implies that something has D if it can manifest, regardless of how that manifestation might come about.

The departure from previously considered views can seem extreme, but Vetter (2015, 64) draws attention to the broad linguistic evidence for this *Possibility* strategy. She cites the Oxford English Dictionary, which says of fragility that it is the property of something which is *'liable to break or be broken; ... easily destroyed'*, and not (for example) *'breaks given a (relatively low) stress'*. Aimar (2019) also shows that in some contexts, 'x is fragile' and 'x can be broken easily' are mutually inferrable, whereas the claims 'x is fragile' and 'if x were hit it would break' are not.

Some have queried whether *all* dispositions can be defined without reference to a stimulus, as per POSSIBILITY. Manley and Wasserman (2008) point out that this is implausible in the case of canonical dispositions like the disposition to break when stressed (though see Vetter 2015 for a reply). Bird (2020) also points out that stimulus conditions are required to distinguish dispositions which have the same manifestation, such as dispositions to break easily for different reasons (e.g., microstructural or circumstantial), or dispositions to generate force in different ways (e.g., charge and mass; see Vetter 2020 for a reply).

Nevertheless, there clearly are benefits to adopting the *Possibility* strategy wholesale, since POSSIBILITY can avoid many of the problems so far considered. Working backwards, analyses of this form do not encounter *Problem #7* disjunctive multi-track dispositions, since they do not define dispositions in terms of tracks at all. All the analysis requires is that a disposed object can manifest *some way or other*; potential stimuli are not relevant to the analysis of the disposition itself. POSSIBILITY also avoids the problem of absent stimuli, since its instances don't even attempt to specify stimuli. Moreover, unspecific stimuli can be accounted for by interpreting the possibility claim causally (e.g., Vetter 2015, 96). For example, *breakability* can be analysed as a possibility to be *caused to break*. Finally, the fact that manifestations need only be possible (rather than inevitable) means that POSSIBILITY's instances are consistent with failures to manifest due to chanciness, masks, and alterers.[23]

Having said all that, theorists who have abandoned the relational strategy (including Vetter and Aimar) seem in agreement that POSSIBILITY can't be the final analysis. A Styrofoam plate in the presence of the hater of Styrofoam *can* break, as can many things, e.g., if using a hydraulic press or as a result of freak chance. The view therefore struggles with mimickers, as it will with tricks and chancy manifestations from undisposed objects. Moreover, there is surely something unsatisfactory about the use of the possibility operator to capture chancy dispositions. A die's disposition to come up with a number between one and five isn't just possible, it is *likely*. POSSIBILITY has no facility to make sense of this. Finally, an issue even more at the forefront of these theorists' minds is the fact that dispositions can come in *degrees*. Consequently, POSSIBILITY represents a point of departure for some theorists towards a quantitative approach to dispositions analysis.

2.4 Quantitative Analyses

Here we look at the problems which have motivated philosophers to introduce some quantitative element to their analyses. As we'll see, this also offers solutions to some of the previous problems.

2.4.1 Problem #8: Dispositional Degrees

The problem of disjunctively multi-track dispositions revealed that things aren't just disposed simpliciter, they come in degrees. As Manley and Wasserman (2007, 69) point out, 'this glass may be simply fragile; but it may also be more fragile than that one. This vase can be simply disposed to break if dropped; but it may also be more disposed to break when dropped than that one.' To compare the degree of objects' dispositions, like their fragility, we can assign them values along a scale ranging from *extremely fragile* to

---

[23] That is, so long as the masks or alters aren't necessary and perfect; cf. Vetter and Busse (2022).

extremely robust. Whether anything on that scale *is fragile* will (we assume) be determined by some context-dependent threshold along that scale.

Dispositional degrees present a problem for all the strategies discussed so far. For example, conditional accounts,

> do not provide a scale corresponding to the set of degrees to which things can have a given disposition. Suppose a is more disposed to break if dropped than b is. This is consistent with each object's being such that it would break if dropped. The difference between them cannot be stated in terms of being such as to break if dropped, which does not come in degrees. And it makes no difference whether the conditional involved in the analysis has been scrupulously refined so as to avoid finks and masks. (Manley and Wasserman 2007, 70)

Moreover, it is also consistent with a being more disposed to break if dropped than b that they both break when dropped (as per the *Generics* strategy), and that both *can break* (as per the *Possibility* strategy). A new strategy is clearly required.

2.4.2 Strategy F: Proportions

In one case, at least, dispositional degrees were the explicit motivation for the introduction of *proportionality* into dispositions analyses (Manley and Wasserman, 2007). The basic idea behind this strategy is that the degree to which objects are disposed corresponds to the proportion of cases in which they manifest.[24] Despite its provenance in the work of Manly and Wassermann, the most straightforward instance of this *Proportionality* strategy is that of Vetter (2011a, 2012, 2014, 2015), who substitutes for the possibility operator in POSSIBILITY a gradable, *object-oriented* possibility operator POT, which Vetter calls 'potentiality'.

> VETTER. For all x, Dx if and only if POT [Mx] to a sufficiently high degree.[25]

Although not all potentialities are dispositions, Vetter claims that all dispositions are potentialities which are had to a sufficiently high degree. Using the possible worlds framework as a heuristic, Vetter suggests that we can understand what it is for something to be fragile in terms of it breaking in a sufficiently large proportion of relevant worlds in which it exists.[26] Correspondingly, we

---

[24] Defenders of this strategy have drawn on Kratzer's (1991) semantic theory for modal expressions to make this idea formally precise.

[25] The details of Vetter's formal treatment of potentiality are vastly more nuanced than we can do justice to here and deserve independent inspection. See especially Vetter (2015, ch. 5).

[26] It is often safe to presume that a world is relevant if it preserves the intrinsic properties of the disposed object. As Vetter admits, however, intrinsicness can't be exactly the criterion for relevance (Vetter 2014, 136–7, fn. 6). The trouble with relevance could, therefore, be a further source of trouble for the account.

can understand something being *more fragile* than something else in terms of it breaking in more relevant worlds (Vetter 2015, 78).[27]

VETTER is a development of POSSIBILITY, and thereby inherits POSSIBILITY's facility for responding to certain problems. However, the introduction of potentiality also enables Vetter's analysis to respond to problems which the *Possibility* strategy is unable to deal with. For instance, even though non-fragile objects can break due to being in mimicking or tricky circumstances, it is reasonable to suppose that the proportion of cases in which they are in those circumstances is relatively low compared with the proportion of cases in which genuinely fragile things break. As a consequence, VETTER does not entail that we should treat just anything which can break as fragile.

At first glance, potentialities also seem to provide a way to develop the treatment of chancy dispositions that makes better sense of the variability of chancy dispositions (Vetter 2011a, 1180, 1184). However, Manley and Wasserman (2011, 1219–20) point out that the use of proportions among worlds to account for probabilistic asymmetries between manifesting and not manifesting (as Vetter's heuristic for potentiality implies) can lead to the requirement for duplicate worlds in some cases. For example, if the trajectory of an electron curving upwards in a magnetic field is half as likely as it is not, then the proportionality account requires that there be exactly two worlds in which it doesn't curve upwards for every one world in which it does. But there is no principled reason to think that not curving upwards gives a world access to exactly twice as many distinct possibilities as curving upwards. All else being equal, the future possibilities for a world in which curving up doesn't occur and a world in which it does are the same (or, if not equal it's at least hard to see why they should be exactly double). If that's right, then the only way to get the right proportions among worlds would seem to be that some worlds (e.g., those in which curving upwards does not occur) are duplicated. However, orthodoxy – and Leibniz's law – tell us that worlds are individuated only by their differences.

For this reason, Manley and Wasserman prefer a more nuanced approach to dispositional degrees in the case of chancy dispositions, requiring that worlds in the modal base be *weighted* according to the chance of manifestation. When fundamental chanciness is relevant to what happens under some stimulus (e.g., a probability 0.33 of curving upwards in a magnetic field) then the associated degree of dispositionality is determined by the proportions of worlds in which

---

[27] In fact, Vetter (2015, 77) suggests that 'cases' (a triple of world, time, and object) might be preferable to possible worlds. Our remarks here should carry over to this alternative interpretation.

manifestation does and doesn't occur weighted by the respective probabilities (e.g., 0.33 and 0.67).

Manley and Wasserman's desire to remain consistent with, though not reliant on, stimulus conditions (due to *Problem #6*) leads them keep a restriction to the more general notion of a 'C-case', which can be interpreted broadly (in the case where there are no stimulus conditions),[28] more narrowly (in the case where there are unspecific stimulus conditions), or more narrowly still (in the case where stimulus conditions are specific). Their preferred schema looks as follows:

> MANWASS. For all x, Dx if and only if Mx in some suitably weighted proportion of C-cases.

Despite their differences, on either VETTER or MANWASS, dispositional degrees are captured in terms of proportions of worlds in which disposed objects manifest. If x is more disposed in way D than y then it will manifest M in a higher proportion of worlds in which it exists than y does. So, for example, if x is highly fragile and y only moderately fragile, then x must break in more (relevant) worlds than y.

As both parties are aware, there are evident problems of principle with this notion of proportionality.

> The set of possible worlds, and a fortiori of cases, is non-denumerably infinite, and so, in all likelihood, are its subsets whose proportions to one another determine fragility. If the proportion of breaking-cases among the relevant cases is to be determined by comparing the cardinality of the respective sets of cases, we are faced with grave and notorious mathematical worries. Proper subsets of non-denumerably infinite sets may have the same cardinality as their supersets; and so no non-trivial comparison of cardinalities may be possible. (Vetter 2015, 77; see Manley and Wasserman 2008, 79–80 for similar remarks)

Both Manley and Wassermann, and Vetter, have made some suggestions for how to get around these worries (Manley and Wasserman 2008, 80–2; Vetter 2014). But one might be concerned that without addressing them fully the proportionality interpretation of dispositional degrees isn't clear enough to provide a workable analysis.

A different issue, applying only to VETTER, is that it is subject to a particular kind of counterexample. Wildman (2020) considers two venomous snakes, one a product of organic evolution and another a product of cybernetic ingenuity. It might well be that the organic snake is more venomous for humans than the

---

[28] Though see Hauska (2015, 169–72) for a criticism of this solution.

cyber snake. But the cyber snake is dependent on humans for its existence, whereas the organic snake is not. Hence, while there will be worlds in which the organic snake can't bring about harm to humans due to an absence of humans, the same can't be said for the cyber snake. Consequently, it could well be that the proportion of worlds in which the cyber snake brings harm to humans, among those worlds in which it exists, is higher than the proportion of worlds in which the organic snake brings about harm to humans, among worlds in which *it* exists (see Vetter 2020, 203–6 for replies; see Aimar 2019, 1684–5 for a similar counterexample and replies).

It is, however, a final problem for both VETTER and MANWASS which leads us to think some other approach to dispositional degrees than proportions among worlds is needed. As Vetter herself seems ready to admit, *x* being *more fragile* than *y* implies, pre-theoretically at least, that it *breaks more easily*. This is clearly not conceptually equivalent to *x* breaking in a higher proportion of instances than *y*. If all fine china vases from the Ming dynasty are encased for their protection by law then they may very well not break as often as the tumblers in my kitchen cupboard, while nevertheless being more fragile. Of course, their encasement doesn't make the Ming vases straightforward to break, but if we take *ease of* breaking to be a matter of the degree of stress required for breaking (as seems natural), they do indeed count as easier to break than the tumblers.

With a suitably diverse modal base the issue just described may be avoided. For VETTER and MANWASS to have a hope of plausibility their corresponding analyses of fragility must concern proportions of manifestation across worlds, including those in which, e.g., there is no legislation protecting Ming vases. But when manifestations also come in degrees this strategy won't work. Consider now the disposition *malleability*. *Any* amount of applied pressure will make an object deform some amount (even if it's imperceptible). So it's unclear how one thing being more malleable than another could be measured in terms of proportions of worlds in which a thing deforms under pressure. More problematic still, no proportionality criterion will be suitable for making sense of the idea that one thing is *twice as malleable* as another. Being twice as malleable presumably means deforming twice as much under the same applied pressure (or deforming the same under half the pressure). But this fact has no bearing on how often a thing deforms, nor does it imply anything directly about which amounts of deformation occur twice as much as other amounts.

It seems to us, then, that the use of proportions in analysis of dispositional degrees, even if only as the go-to heuristic, cannot be quite what is required. Another strategy is needed.

2.4.3 Strategy G: Fine-Graining

A different analysis, which also employs quantitative methods for dealing with dispositional degrees, is provided by Aimar (2019). Like VETTER, Aimar's analysis takes POSSIBILITY as its point of departure. It therefore inherits POSSIBILITY's ability to respond to problems of masks, alters, absent and unspecific stimuli, and disjunctively multi-track dispositions. However, instead of modifying the modal operator in order to deal with dispositional degrees, Aimar advises that the *manifestation* be understood as more fine-grained, which we denote by the addition of an asterisk as follows:

AIMAR. For all x, if and only if Dx then there is some world in which M$^*x$.

Whereas preceding analyses of fragility took the relevant manifestation to be *breaking*, Aimar encourages us to take manifestation to be a *variable* which takes different degrees of ease of breaking in different contexts (fragile will mean breaking easily in some contexts, breaking extraordinarily easily in others). Comparison of dispositional degrees of fragility can therefore be understood in terms of different degrees of ease of breaking. Hence, that x is more fragile than y means that x breaks more easily than y, where ease of breaking might be captured on a gradable scale of quantity of stress required. Therefore, similarly to Vetter's handling of unspecific stimuli, the relevance of applied stress to whether something is fragile (and by how much) is brought back in as a qualification on the manifestation behaviour. But again, like VETTER, the approach doesn't demand that degrees of manifestation *must* be captured by reference to a cause. For instance, whether one isotope is more disposed to radioactively decay than another might be captured in terms of the values of fundamental probabilities for those decays.

But it is important to make clear the novelty of Aimar's *Fine-graining* strategy. As we saw, Vetter made much of the fact that dictionary definitions of dispositions like fragility emphasise the ease of some or other manifestation. Vetter's proposal interprets this ease as a qualification on the relevant modality.[29] By contrast, Aimar suggests that it is instead the *manifestation* which gets qualified. It thereby avoids many of the particular interpretive issues that the *Proportionality* strategy faces.

The *Fine-graining* strategy is a promising way to capture dispositional degrees. Yet we might be concerned that it doesn't go far enough. As it stands, the strategy only has scope for one dimension of fine-graining. Ease of breaking,

---

[29] For Vetter, this is the sui generis modality of potentiality, which can be understood via the heuristic of proportions of possible worlds.

for instance, is naturally captured in terms of degree of applied stress. Objects are therefore more or less fragile if they require, respectively, more or less stress to break them. But we also take there to be a clear sense in which the *amount of breaking* is relevant to how fragile something is. More generally, the degree of dispositionality doesn't just concern how much stimulus is required to get an equivalent manifestation, but also how much manifestation is produced by equivalent stimuli. To put things in these terms is to go beyond anything expressible with AIMAR's form.

Moreover, the *Proportionality* strategy enabled some responses that the *Fine-graining* strategy does not. Both VETTER and MANWASS avoid the problem of mimickers and tricks by relying on the idea that even though some objects will mimic dispositions, and others will be dispositional tricks, their proportion of manifestations across all the relevant worlds is low enough to prohibit them from counting as instances of the disposition. AIMAR can't appeal to this idea. In order to avoid counting those mimicking and tricky cases we could try putting restrictions on the relevant possible worlds in which manifestation occurs, or else by further fine-graining the manifestation. But it's far from clear how such specifications could work in a non-trivial way. All things considered, we are still not quite there with the ideal strategy. And, there still remains one last problem case to consider.

2.4.4 Problem #9: Conjunctive Multi-Track Dispositions

Even if we fix on one determinate degree of fragility (e.g., mean-average fragility) there remain quantitative considerations which have so far been ignored. Striking a (moderately) fragile vase can often lead it to break. But, as we've seen, how hard one strikes it (e.g., whether it is bumped, knocked, hit, thwacked, crushed, or pulverised) will likely influence how it breaks. Moreover, as we've just pointed out in critiquing the *Fine-graining* strategy, the manifestation behaviour of (mean-average) fragility can be rendered in more varied terms than simply *breaking* (under varying stresses). For example, for any of the various applied stresses, a fragile object can chip, split, fracture, shatter, atomise, or plasmarise.

From the perspective of a traditional conditionals approach to analysing dispositions, observations like these can seem to commit us to a multitude of conditionals for any determinate (non-disjunctively multi-track) disposition. For they imply that 'there is a whole set of pairs of triggering [stimulus] conditions T_i and manifestations M_i, such that an object b with [the disposition] would manifest M_i if it were in condition T_i' (Kistler 2012, 134). Specifically, these features show that the relevant disposition is *conjunctively multi-track*, since any instance of the disposition will need to satisfy each of the associated counterfactual relationships or 'tracks'.[30]

Quantified science provides a large repository of conjunctive multi-track dispositions. Often the more specific stimulus and manifestation properties are related by a 'characterising equation' (Friend 2021) or law. For example, having a certain value of conductivity means exhibiting certain current densities under a proportional electrical field according to Ohm's law (cf. Kistler 2012). Likewise, having a certain specific heat capacity means exhibiting certain changes in temperature under proportional heat absorption according to the specific heat formula; having a certain carrying capacity means exhibiting certain rates of change in the population of an inhabiting organism with a particular growth rate according to the logistic growth formula; having a certain price elasticity means exhibiting certain changes in demand given changes in the price of a commodity according to the equation for price elasticity; and so on. In each case, the 'track' relating some determinate value of stimulus to a determinate value of manifestation seems to be part of the behavioural characterisation of the quantitative multi-track disposition.

The extra detail of these counterfactual relationships is easily incorporated within SEMs. To accommodate the multi-track details for the case of fragility, all we need to do is redefine the variables from our earlier example in subsection 2.1, as in Table 6 (NB: the structural equation and causal graph have not changed).

No doubt this SEM provides only one possible way of giving a conjunctively multi-track interpretation of fragility. Unlike the cases from quantitative science just mentioned, the disposition of fragility itself likely does not entail any *specific* functional relationship between the variables characterised in Table 6. Indeed, this is a straightforward consequence of the fact that fragility is (as we saw above) *disjunctively* multi-track as well. Presumably, much the same will go for other 'everyday' dispositions like solubility, malleability, courageousness, etc. In each case, however, there are clearly some constraints on what any function *could* be if our conception of these dispositions were to be precisified. For instance, we know that fragile objects are such that increases in applied stress are correlated with increases in degree of breaking.

The entailment by a disposition of limits on any range of plausible functions relating degrees of stimulus and manifestation confers more complexity on its

---

[30] Note the contrast with disjunctively multi-track dispositions which are such that different instances satisfy different tracks.

Table 6 Details for a causal model for conjunctive multi-track fragility

Variables			Structural equations
Symbol	**Possible values**	**Interpretation**	
FR	1	*x* is fragile	(Exogenous)
	0	*x* is not fragile	
ST	6	*x* is pulverised	(Exogenous)
	5	*x* is crushed	
	4	*x* is thwacked	
	3	*x* is hit	
	2	*x* is knocked	
	1	*x* is bumped	
	0	*x* undergoes no stress (at all)	
BR	6	*x* plasmarises	$BR \Leftarrow FR \times ST$
	5	*x* atomises	
	4	*x* shatters	
	3	*x* fractures	
	2	*x* splits	
	1	*x* chips	
	0	*x* does not break (at all)	

analysis than permitted by any of the strategies so far considered. Other than AIMAR, no analysis so far considered supplied more than a single manifestation or stimulus per disposition. AIMAR's invocation of more fine-grained and, crucially, *gradable* manifestations is clearly an improvement in that regard. But it still isn't sufficient to deal with conjunctively multi-track dispositions, which exhibit both gradable manifestations *and stimuli*. Nor would it be enough to simply recognise fine-grained stimuli in the analysis alongside fine-grained manifestations. An analysis which properly addresses conjunctively multi-track dispositions must show *how each possible degree of stimulus is connected to some specific manifestation* (or at least would be under some precisification of their functional relationship).[31]

---

[31] Consider Oobleck (a mixture of cornstarch and water), a fluid which exhibits high tensile strength when subject to significant impact but behaves like a liquid under more moderate pressure. Oobleck will break when subject to the right kind of weak applied stress, and it reacts differently under different applied stresses. Oobleck is, therefore, conjunctively multi-track and plausibly relates precisely the same range of values of applied stress to degrees of breaking as fragile objects. Nevertheless, oobleck isn't fragile, we suggest, precisely because it fails to exhibit the right functional relationships. While fragile objects break more easily under greater stresses, oobleck breaks less easily (within some salient range).

2.4.5 Strategy H: Potentials for Functions

We are aware of two attempts to deal with conjunctively multi-track dispositions. We discuss one in this section, the other will form the basis of our novel
strategy in the next section.

Vetter discusses conjunctively multi-track dispositions in the specific context
of *nomological dispositions*, those quantitative scientific dispositions which
have clear characterising equations.[32] Since Vetter favours a possibility view
of dispositions (see POSSIBILTY, subsection 2.3.5 and VETTER, subsection
2.4.2), her analysis of them is not in terms of the conditional implications of
manifestation given stimulus, let alone a multiplicity of such implications.
Nevertheless, and unlike her preferred treatment of non-conjunctively multi-
track dispositions, Vetter does retain the link between the putative stimulus
property and manifestation.[33] She does this by suggesting that the manifestations of conjunctively multi-track dispositions are the *entire functional relationship* specified by the relevant nomological equation. In this way, the
putative stimulus is brought inside the potentiality operator to embellish the
manifestation condition as follows (Vetter 2015, 61, 284):

FUNCPOT. For all x, Dx if and only if POT $[M(x) = f(S(x))]$.

So, for example, Vetter's analysis of the disposition of having elementary
charge (e Coulombs) is given as follows (Vetter 2015, 61):[34]

ELECPOT. For all x, x has charge e if and only if POT [For all r and Q, if x is
distance r from a charge of q then $F_E = keQ/r^2$].

Vetter points out that if this *Potentials for Functions* strategy is to ensure the
metaphysical necessity of laws, the potentiality for nomological dispositions
like elementary charge will have to be *maximal*, i.e., manifesting in every
member of the relevant modal base.[35] This could be cause for concern. First,
it means that in the case of such dispositions, POT plays the same role as
a necessity operator, providing another major contrast among types of

---

[32] For the sake of our exposition, we treat nomological potentialities as dispositions (rather than
powers), though both we, and Vetter, would want to say her example of elementary charge is an
ontic property. This shouldn't undermine our reasoning since our critique of Vetter's analysis in
general.

[33] A dispositionalist could, perhaps, coherently maintain that the functional relationships are not
part of the analysis of the corresponding disposition. We, like Vetter, find that implausible. Being
electrically charged is not merely to supply an attractive force in response to the presence of other
charges, it is to supply a force given by the Coulomb force law, or some refinement thereof.

[34] We're not sure that elementary charge is a disposition – we suspect it's a power (but see footnote
32).

[35] Although many fans of dispositional analyses of laws of nature take laws to be metaphysically
necessary, Vetter herself remains open to their contingency (see Vetter 2015, 289).

disposition within Vetter's overall system. Second, the maximal potentiality attributed to dispositions like elementary charge renders the analysans in ELECPOT logically equivalent to a plurality of necessary counterfactuals. So, for dispositions which need analysing in terms of maximal potentialities for functions, there is not any logical distinction between Vetter's preferred approach and one which advocates for a plurality of conditionals in the analysans. But Vetter is at pains to distance herself from a conditionals approach to analysis.

The *Potentials for Functions* strategy for conjunctively multi-track dispositions would cease to be akin to a conditionals approach if the potentialities involved were less than maximal. And Vetter (2015, 288) suggests that less-than-maximal potentialities might be appropriate in the case of idealisation laws. However, there is reason to be sceptical that this is the right treatment of idealisation. It is not the case, for example, that the ideal gas equation is an accurate description of gases in many but not all cases, as a less-then-maximal potentiality for the ideal gas equation would imply. Rather, the ideal gas law isn't accurate in *any* cases. This is because, as with most idealising laws, there are interferences (e.g., from particle sizes and mutual attraction) which are necessarily present. What makes the ideal gas law a law is not that it's exactly right in some cases, but that it captures some of the relevant causally relevant properties in *all* cases (Friend 2022b).[36]

The limitation in dealing with idealisation laws may not seem too disastrous for the *Potentials for Functions* strategy, so long as it can handle strict lawlike dispositions (like elementary charge) and everyday conjunctively multi-track dispositions (like fragility). However, we think the limitation reveals a broader issue for everyday dispositions too. The issue hinges on the kinds of function we envisage entering the analysis of everyday conjunctively multi-track dispositions. We know from the *Getting Specific* strategy that to make particular masks and alterers explicit would be to put too much into the analysans. Fragility, therefore, should *not* be analysed by the maximal potential for some functional relationship which includes variables for all possible interferences. But we also suggest that failing to say anything at all about the relationship between stimulus and manifestation when masks or alterers are present would be to put in too little. The possibility for interference on an object's fragility should not force an analysis to say nothing about what happens in these cases but should only force the analysis to be less specific about the causal influence

---

[36] At this point, Vetter might remind us that the interpretation of potentiality in terms of proportions of worlds is a 'formal model and rough approximation'. But with no other interpretation of proportionality forthcoming we may feel within our rights to look elsewhere for an analysis which does so. (Vetter does suggest that the probability calculus could serve as an alternative formalism to understand proportionality, but this would seem to encounter the same issue.)

applied stress has on breaking. After all, when something is fragile, it's not that wrapping it in bubble wrap means we have no idea about how applied stresses will affect whether it breaks; typically, we know just that it will now be *harder* to break under stress. FUNCPOT offers no means to do this, since it states that disposed objects will either behave exactly according to the embedded function or else behave in such a way that the analysis is completely silent on which causal influences are present. However, we think there is a different strategy which permits navigation between these options.

2.5 Structural Equations Analyses

Our reason for introducing SEMs early on wasn't just for presentational purposes. It seems to us that structural equations might well serve as central components in analyses of dispositions which avoid many of the problem cases raised above. Limitations on space prevent us from developing an entirely new account (though see Friend unpublished manuscript); however, we present the core idea, captured in a 'Simple Structural Equations Analysis' and show how it neatly deals with several of the foregoing problem cases. After considering an objection to the approach, we then suggest, in outline, various amendments to deal with the remaining problem cases.

2.5.1 Strategy I: Simple Structural Equations Analysis (SSEA)

Our simple structural equations analysis has the following schema:

SSEA. For all x, if and only if $D(x) = d$ then $M(x) \Leftarrow f(S(x))$.

Let's draw attention to two things straight away. First, what gets explicitly analysed is the value of a 'disposition variable' $D(x)$, as opposed to the respective qualitative disposition D (which does not come in degrees). This makes the analysis amenable to dealing with *Problem #8: Dispositional Degrees*, since how much something is disposed in way D will be explicit in the analysandum. For example, with a fine-grained conception of fragility, SSEA permits an analysis of being *very fragile, extremely fragile, moderately fragile*, etc. (assuming these degrees can be treated as values of a well-ordered variable). But SSEA does not preclude analysis of a purely qualitative conception of fragility. For that we interpret the variable as a binary 'dummy variable', and the schematic analysans $D(x) = d$ would be replaced by the fragility variable being assigned the value 1 (as opposed to 0).[37]

---

[37] As in subsection 2.1.2, we follow the convention of representing the instantiation of a qualitative property, like fragility, with a 1 and the failure to instantiate the property with a 0.

Second, the analysans takes the form of a structural equation relating the causal influence of a stimulus variable on the manifestation variable, via a function f. This function is effectively a characterisation of *the way the stimulus variable affects the manifestation variable given the disposition* $D(x) = d$. That is, the function is logically determined by the specific value assignment of the disposition. As before, the resulting structural equation encodes *multiple* counterfactuals. The minimum number of counterfactuals encoded is in the case where $D(x), M(x)$ and $S(x)$ are dichotomous. In that case the functional relationship reduces to a unit coefficient and $M(x) \Leftarrow f(S(x))$ encodes two counterfactuals, one 'positive' and one 'negative':

> POSITIVE. If x were stimulated $(S(x) = 1)$ then x would manifest $(M(x) = 1)$.
>
> NEGATIVE. If x were not stimulated $(S(x) = 0)$ then x would not manifest $(M(x) = 0)$.

Notice that by encoding both conditionals, SSEA can deal with *Problem #4: Tricks*. That problem effectively showed that the associated POSITIVE conditionals – those employed in instances of SCA – can be true in cases where the disposition isn't instantiated because the manifestation is liable to happen anyway (e.g., when a non-fragile object is about to be crushed in a hydraulic press). However, in these 'tricky' instances it is never the case that the associated NEGATIVE conditional also holds. If the object is not fragile, it is *not* the case that if it weren't to undergo applied stress it would not break, because it *would still* break due to the hydraulic press (the same reasoning applies to Contessa's example of the mug of cooling coffee).

If the variables $S(x)$ and $M(x)$ take more than two values, the number of counterfactuals encoded will be greater. In general, there is a counterfactual encoded for every possible stimulus value. This ensures that the schema for analysis can, in principle at least, respond to *Problem #9: Conjunctive Multi-Track Dispositions*. For instance, under SSEA the analysis of electric charge is as follows:

> ELECSE. For all x, if and only if $Q(x) = e$ then $F_E(x) \Leftarrow keQ(y)/r(x,y)^2$.

ELECSE appears to place the same necessary and sufficient conditions on a charged object as ELECPOT. However, unlike Vetter's two-schema analysis (VETTER and FUNCPOT), by being expressed in terms of a structural equation (an array of counterfactual conditionals) ELECSE has the unique benefit of providing a *unified treatment* of conjunctive multi-track dispositions and purely qualitative dispositions like the coarse-grained conception of fragility.

2.5.2 An Objection: Too Many Counterfactuals?

Before considering more complex analysis in terms of structural equations we want first to address, up front, one worry about their use: that having a disposition shouldn't entail so many counterfactuals. There are two variants of this worry. The first is that, while it is common practice to analyse dispositions in terms of the POSITIVE conditional (or some variation thereof), the additional NEGATIVE conditional is unreasonable.

Our response to this concern is more fully worked out elsewhere (Friend unpublished manuscript), but the gist of it draws on the fact that both conditionals are essential for a counterfactual treatment of causal relations (cf. Lewis 1973a). This treatment capitalises on the observation that, except in circumstances where causes pre-empt another potential cause, their effects counterfactually *depend* on those causes. Negative conditionals (concerning when events do not occur) are an essential component in characterising this dependency. Since being a cause of manifestation is (save some recalcitrant examples, see footnote 7) a defining characteristic of dispositions' stimuli, it therefore seems inevitable that NEGATIVE will need to feature in the analysis unless the very employment of counterfactuals is to be replaced entirely with some different causal treatment.

As observed, there are cases in which causes pre-empt others. In those cases the NEGATIVE conditional is false. So the vase, which is actually fragile and caused to break by applied stress, might be in a situation where it would have broken anyway due (for example) to a hydraulic press (see Contessa 2016 for another example involving Leo the chameleon). But we see no structural difference here to cases in which the POSITIVE conditional is falsified due to masks. In either case, some external factor means that a counterfactual which is central to the analysis is rendered false. So, the concern with NEGATIVE is right insofar as it shows that the SSEA cannot be quite right. But that's not because of the addition of the conditional into the characterisation per se. Rather, it's because both POSITIVE and NEGATIVE are subject to a generalised problem of masks.

We're about to offer a solution to that problem. Before that, there is a second source of concern about the volume of counterfactuals being introduced which we should address. Recall that we objected to the *Strategy A: Getting Specific* approach on the grounds that the analyses of dispositions it demanded would be overly complex. The SSEA schema can seem guilty of just the same issue. For it requires that the technical formalism of structural equations, which allows for an infinity of conditionals to be encoded, be built right into dispositions analyses. To assuage this concern, it's worth highlighting the distinction between analyses which predict that mastery of a concept involves patterns of reasoning tacitly implemented in cognition, which are more technically complex than we are typically aware of, and analyses which demand that mastery of a concept or ability require knowledge of some endless list of disparate conditions. While the former demand is invoked in the cognitive sciences, the latter are rightly avoided. The *Getting Specific* strategy recommends analyses which arguably cannot be conceptually grasped due to being necessarily so expansive. But SSEA can be concisely expressed, albeit in a formalism rarely made explicit, and so could be reasonably implemented tacitly in cognition.

2.5.3 SEMs, Masks, and Alters

We just saw that pre-empting causes lead to the falsity of certain counterfactuals encoded in the structural equations of SSEAs. Of course, it would be disastrous to the general SEM framework if pre-emption cases could not be modelled. Happily, they can be (Halpern and Pearl 2005). When two potential cause variables A and B of an effect variable C are such that if $A = 1$ it will pre-empt $B = 1$ as the cause of $C = 1$, then the structural equation for C must simply include *both* variables, i.e., $C \Leftarrow A + B - AB$.

As predicted by our response to the foregoing objection, this is exactly what happens in cases demonstrating *Problem #1: Masks*. When further interfering factors, like a mask, are present, the structural equation governing the manifestation variable (e.g., the harm done to an agent $H(agent)$) is a function of the relevant disposition (e.g., the poisonousness $P(x)$ of the poison), the stimulus (e.g., whether the poison is ingested $I(x)$) *and also the mask* (e.g., whether an antidote accompanies x, $A(x)$). Hence, if we knew exactly what masks would occur, and how they influenced the manifestation variable, we might include them as further variables in the SEM.

Now, the discussion of the *Potentials for Functions* strategy and the *Getting Specific* strategy should have persuaded us that including all possible interfering factors in an analysing equation is implausible. What we *can* do, however, is draw attention to the fact that the stimulus variable *will feature in whatever function does happen to characterise exactly all the influencing factors* (including the stimulus) on a manifestation variable. This can be rendered as follows:

SSEA*. For all x, $D(x) = d$ if and only if $M(x) \Leftarrow f\left(S(x), \ldots\right)$.

The structural equation SSEA* is like SSEA, but the analysing function has been embellished by ellipses to indicate further potential causal variables. By characterising a disposition this way, SSEA*s lose the ability to encode counterfactuals about determinate values of variables. Yet they are not entirely trivial, either. For instance, the schema tells us that having the disposition is a necessary and sufficient condition for the stimulus variable *being one of the influences* on the manifestation variable. It therefore provides a significant constraint on whatever more accurate SEM involving the manifestation variable would look like.[38] It is just this middle position which we advised in critiquing the *Potentials for Functions* strategy. Unlike that strategy, the employment of structural equations recommended here allows that the causal influence of stimulus can still be recognised even when masks are present, but without having to be specific about which masks those might be. Note also that while the analysans incorporates an open-ended function, the analysans itself is not open-ended (as it was argued it would have to be if the *Getting Specific* strategy was to work). As before, whereas the *Getting Specific* strategy recommends an analysans which cannot be expressed concisely (because every eventuality has to be made explicit), SSEA*'s analysans *can* be expressed concisely: the manifestation variable is causally determined by a function over some set of variables which includes the stimulus variable.

As it turns out, this strategy also helps address *Problem #2: Alterers* (subsection 2.2.2). Not only might masking variables appear in a more explicit structural equation for circumstances involving a disposition, the disposition variable itself might also do so. Of course, we must omit the disposition variable from the structural equation featuring in the analysans (our goal is to give noncircular conditions for the instantiation of the disposition variable). Nevertheless, it remains true that the disposition variable is an influence on manifestation. This much is clear from the fact that there is a directed edge from the disposition variable to the manifestation variable in each of the causal graphs we've considered. Alterers are stimulus variables which influence the manifestation variable *and* the disposition variable. That means the disposition variable $D(x)$ can't be assumed to retain the value d under any value of $S(x)$. Unlike SSEA, SSEA* implicitly allows for variation in further influences on the manifestation variable (such as from the disposition variable itself) and is therefore not falsified by such factors.

2.5.4 Dealing with Remaining Problems

The structural equation SSEA* offers a way of responding to many of the problem cases considered throughout this section. However, some problems

---

[38] In fact, we can be more specific even than this, since we typically know that the particular way in which the stimulus influences the manifestation variable will remain constant. More specifically, we know that the manifestation variable is governed by a structural equation which has some particular function over the stimulus as a 'special case', i.e., where further variables are set to constants (cf. Friend unpublished manuscript).

remain unaddressed and we have some ideas about further developments which might help (see Friend unpublished manuscript for a more detailed explication).

Briefly, we suggest that *Problem #7: Disjunctive Multi-Track Dispositions* (subsection 2.3.4) can be addressed by permitting some restricted variation in the function which takes values of the stimulus (and potentially other variables) to manifestation values. Unlike the disposition *having elemental charge*, the disposition *being fragile* doesn't entail any specific function from applied stress to degree of breaking. But, as we acknowledged, it does plausibly entail a limited range of possible functions, e.g., only those in which increases of applied stress lead to increases in degree of breaking. We therefore suggest that analysis of these dispositions should proceed by restricting the functions to ones of this general type rather than to any single function.

Problem #6: Unspecific Stimuli (subsection 2.3.3) can be dealt with in a similar manner by permitting variation in stimuli. At its broadest, the analysis can simply quantify over all possible stimulus variables. Breakability, for instance, would be analysed in terms of the existence of *some or other stimulus variable* which can feature in a function which maps to degrees of breaking.

Problem #5: Chancy Dispositions (subsection 2.3.1) could be dealt with in one of two ways. One would be to admit error terms into the analysing structural equations. Such terms could take a range of values consistent with possible variation in the manifestation variable due to chancy interference. Perhaps a better solution, however, would be to substitute for the manifestation variable a variable which ranges over probability distributions of the manifestation variable. That way, the analysing structural equation would not map to possible values of manifestation, but possible distributions.

Finally, *Problem #3: Mimickers* (subsection 2.2.3) is, we think, probably best analysed via the understanding that mimickers come about through deviant causal chains. Dispositions, we take it, imply some specific mechanism by which stimulus results in manifestation. As is clear from Figure 4, mimickers work by other, deviant, means. Having said that, we're not sure how exactly to specify constraints on the right mechanism without getting more specific in the analysis than we think is ultimately plausible. One possible route is to capitalise on the idea that dispositions which are subject to mimickers should be considered as *realiser functional properties* rather than role functional. In that case, the disposition is understood as identical to the empirically discoverable causal base rather than a second-order property defined in terms of having some such base (see Section 1). Crucially, such an identity would be a posteriori and so need not be known purely from competency with the dispositional concept.

A legitimate concern with the suggested solutions to these problems is that it forces the analyses of dispositions to go pluralist. That's something we (and the authors we've engaged with) have generally tried to avoid. Nevertheless, the pluralism invoked is, for the most part, within the rough framework identified by the SSEA schema. Most of the relevant differences come down to how specific we make the structural equation on the right-hand side. Nevertheless, it's not clear that this extends to our proposed solution to the problem of mimickers. Perhaps, in the end, some pluralism cannot be avoided.

2.6 Summary

In this section we've considered a variety of analyses of dispositional properties. Although we have highlighted some of the problems facing each of the broad strategies discussed in Sections 2.1–2.4 it's fair to say that the viability of each of them is currently being explored by philosophers. We've also taken the opportunity to propose a new approach to dispositions' analyses involving structural equations. Despite its relative novelty, we hope the potential of this approach has been made more plausible by our demonstration of the relevance of structural equations modelling techniques throughout this section. The applicability of these techniques to highlight the causal subtleties of dispositions suggests that the techniques themselves can enable a strategy for analysis which avoids many of the traditional counterexamples.

It should be recalled that in analysing dispositions, and the causal relations they enter into, we have avoided passing any judgement on the nature of those causal relations. Whether dispositions and their causal relations are grounded in categorical properties, powers, or something else entirely is orthogonal to the discussion engaged in so far. By contrast, the next section engages directly with this topic.

3 Powers

3.1 Introduction

The previous section concerned dispositions and dispositional behaviour (here we will use 'dispositions' as a shorthand catch-all for 'dispositions and dispositional behaviour'). This section concerns what metaphysically explains the presence of dispositions and related phenomena such as laws of nature and modality. The suggestion to be explored is that *ontic* properties explain dispositions and these properties are what we call *powers*. For a property to be *ontic*, remember, is for it to be a genuine constituent of our ontology – something that exists in the world independently of our thought and language. The section is structured around four closely related questions about powers:

1. What *is* a power?
2. Why should we accept the existence of powers?

3. How should we understand the metaphysics of powers?
4. How far does the powers ontology extend?

Here is a flavour of what is to come. Powers are (at least) properties that are necessarily connected with dispositions; powers are to be understood in contrast with the 'Humean' view that properties are modally separate from the dispositions that they confer (Section 3.2). We should accept the existence of powers so conceived because they hold the promise of explaining other phenomena of philosophical interest (Section 3.3). However, being necessarily connected with dispositions is only a necessary condition on powers being able to do good explanatory work. So, more needs to be said about how these necessary connections arise, and hence about the details of the metaphysics of powers, in order to ensure that they satisfy the explanatory aspirations of their advocates (Sections 3.4 and 3.5). Finally, we will show that which properties get to count as powers depends on the metaphysics of the powers that one adopts (Section 3.6).

3.2 What Is a Power?

Debates about *powers* can be understood as part of the project of investigating the metaphysics of properties. But this requires further qualification. There are (at least) two dimensions along which one may investigate the metaphysics of properties. One of these dimensions concerns whether properties exist independently of propertied individuals (proponents of Platonic universals say they do; nominalists, trope theorists, and proponents of Aristotelian universals say they do not).[39] Another dimension of the question about the metaphysics of properties concerns the relationship between the properties that individuals instantiate and how those propertied individuals are *disposed*.[40] It is this latter issue with which powers theorists are concerned.

To get a grip on what powers theorists have to say about the relationship between properties and dispositions, it helps to contrast the powers metaphysic with *Humeanism*. Metaphysicians of a *Humean* persuasion endorse the idea (sometimes called *Hume's Dictum*, see, e.g., Wilson 2010) that there are no necessary connections between distinct existences.[41] A corollary of this is that there are no necessary connections between the distinct properties that

---

[39] An interesting issue, though one that we do not have space to consider here, is whether/to what extent different accounts of properties (Platonism, nominalism, Aristotelianism) are compatible with different accounts of powers; see, e.g., Vogt (2022); Whittle (2009).

[40] It has been argued that these two dimensions of the question about the metaphysics of powers are related, e.g., by Coates (2022); Tugby (2013, 2022a).

[41] The sense of necessity here and throughout (unless otherwise specified) is the sense in which if it is necessary that P, there really is no sense in which it is possible that not-P. This is what one might call *absolute* necessity (Hale 2002, 299), or *metaphysical* necessity (Williamson 2013, 3).

individuals instantiate and how those individuals are disposed, and hence no necessary connections between individuals by virtue of the properties that they instantiate. For example, individuals that instantiate *mass* are disposed to warp spacetime. It follows that any two distinct massive individuals, *m1* and *m2*, (situated in spacetime) are disposed to accelerate towards each other. But the Humean denier of necessary connections will maintain that the property *mass* and the disposition to warp spacetime nonetheless *could* come apart; it is possible that something instantiated mass and yet is not disposed to warp spacetime (see, e.g., Lewis 2009; Schaffer 2005). Hence it is *possible* that *m1* and *m2* were not disposed to accelerate towards each other (even assuming that they continued to instantiate mass and be situated in spacetime). Humeans then endorse a metaphysics of properties that ensures this modal separability of properties and dispositions so as to exclude necessary connections between properties and dispositions and between distinct propertied individuals, thus upholding Hume's Dictum.

Powers theorists, by contrast, are happy to admit necessary connections. In particular, they are happy to admit necessary connections between properties and dispositions and any necessary connections thus induced between distinct individuals in virtue of their dispositional properties.[42] This, in turn, is related to powers theorists' interest in *explaining* dispositions in terms of powers. In very broad terms, then: *powers are properties that necessitate dispositions.*[43]

We'd like to emphasise that it is a *necessary* condition on a property being a power that it necessitates certain dispositions,[44] though this may not be a *sufficient* condition on what it is to be a power because powers theorists typically also think that the necessary connections must come about in such a way that powers *explain* the dispositions with which they are necessarily connected. This is consistent with the broadly functionalist understanding of the relation between powers and dispositions that we sketched in Section 1, but it adds more detail about the relationship between the properties (powers) and the dispositions that they realise.

What *suffices* for a property to be a power is a vexed issue, one that is intimately tied up with the account of how the necessary connections between powers and dispositions arise. This will be a key discussion point in Sections 3.4 and 3.5.

---

[42] After all, why should we accept Hume's Dictum and why think that contingency reigns supreme? Why not think that contingency is just as hard earned as necessity? (cf. Heil 2015; Kimpton-Nye 2021c).

[43] 'Powers' and 'dispositions' are sometimes used interchangeably in the literature, but recall that we are distinguishing these two notions: see Section 1 for details.

[44] This is what Bird (2016; 2018) calls *Modal Fixity*.

There is a strand of thought in the literature according to which powers ought to be primarily understood in terms of *real activity*: 'From this perspective, to say that things in the world have causal powers . . . is to say that things engage in activity, are able to *do*. Reality, we might say (from this perspective) is thus genuinely, irreducibly, non-metaphorically dynamic' (Groff 2021, 4) (see also Ellis 2001, 2002; Mumford and Anjum 2011). If, as we suggest, powers are properties that are necessarily connected with dispositions and the latter are a variety of real activity, then one might think that the present suggestion is consistent with, e.g., Groff's view.

However, we would prefer not to prejudge the question of realism about *activity* in our characterisation of powers. There is reason to believe that *real activity* is inconsistent with *eternalism* (understood as the view that all times, past, present, and future, exist and are equally real) because the latter looks quite *static*. But we do not think that the powers metaphysic should have such direct implications for the metaphysics of time (for discussion, see, e.g., Backmann 2018; Friebe 2018; Donati 2018; Giannini 2022 – the latter argues that powers characterised in terms of real activity or dynamicity are in fact compatible with eternalism). What's more, it has been argued (Kimpton-Nye 2018, 2021; Leech 2017) that in order to be *extensionally adequate* a powers-based account of modality (e.g., Borghini and Williams 2008; Jacobs 2010; Vetter 2015) ought to be twinned with eternalism.

Hence, in characterising powers, we prefer to put the emphasis on there being a necessary connection between properties and dispositions. This characterisation may be understood as irreducibly modal twice over: there is a *necessary* connection between property and *disposition*, where neither the necessary connection nor the dispositional modality is to be reduced to anything non-modal (though perhaps the latter can be reduced to some other modal notion such as the counterfactual or possibility, see Section 2). In our opinion, this is plenty anti-Humean enough to count as a *powers* view.[45]

Powers, then, are properties that are necessarily connected with the dispositions that they confer upon their bearers. But this raises further questions. *Why* think that properties and dispositions are necessarily connected? *How* do these necessary connections come about? These questions will be the focus of the next two sections, which will also address the question of what *suffices* for a property to be a power.

---

[45] Maudlin (2007) endorses a view of *laws* as 'productive', which one may view as an analogue of an account of powers in terms of *real activity*, that he twins with eternalism. But this also seems like a strange combination (see Chen and Goldstein 2022, 17)

3.3 Powers, Huh? What Are They Good for?

We will now describe three areas of philosophical work to which powers have been put: accounting for the identities of properties, accounting for laws of nature, and accounting for modality. This is a far from exhaustive survey, but these issues have featured particularly prominently in the literature on powers.

Each of these areas of philosophical work for powers requires (at least) that: *there exist necessary connections between powers and dispositions* and the latter two (laws of nature and modality) explicitly require that powers also metaphysically *explain* dispositions. Hence, the point of this section is to motivate the minimal account of what it is to be a power, sketched above in Section 3.2, before investigating in more detail how to understand the metaphysics of powers, if powers really are to be *explanatory* in the ways desired (Sections 3.4 and 3.5).

3.3.1 Property Identity, Scepticism, and Science-Friendliness

One prominent reason for thinking that properties are necessarily connected with dispositions is dissatisfaction with the metaphysics of properties required to uphold Hume's Dictum. This subsection will sketch the Humean view of properties, problems for that view, and how this relates to admitting necessary connections between properties and dispositions.

Properties, according to the Humean, are *quiddities*. Black (2000, 92), uses 'quidditism' for 'the acceptance of primitive identity between fundamental qualities across possible worlds' (see also Lewis 2009, 209). Thus, on this view, for any two distinct properties, $P1$ and $P2$, according to the quidditist, no more can be said about what individuates $P1$ and $P2$ than that $P1$ is the property that it is and $P2$ is the property that it is and that it is not the case that $P1 = P2$. Crucially for our purposes, this entails that the *dispositions* with which we may associate *mass*, for example, such as a disposition to warp spacetime, are in no way tied up with what it is to be mass. The same goes, *mutatis mutandis,* for other properties.

It helps to draw some finer distinctions here. The view according to which there is nothing more to a property than primitive self-identify and distinctness from other properties is what Smith (2016) has called I-quidditism (individuation quidditism), which she distinguishes from the view that she calls R-quidditism (recombinatorial quidditism) according to which 'there are no restrictions on the recombination of properties in metaphysically possible worlds' (Smith 2016, 240). In other words, R-quidditism says that the connections between properties and dispositions are thoroughly contingent. It is plausible that I-quidditism is a necessary (but not sufficient) condition for R-quidditism (Smith 2016, 240). Hence, it is in the interest of satisfying this necessary condition on the denial of necessary connections between properties and dispositions (as per R-quidditism) that the Humean wishes to uphold I-quidditism. In short, Humeans maintain that properties are quiddities in both the individuative and recombinatorial senses: there is nothing more to what it is to be a given property than primitive self-identity and distinctness from other properties, and properties are free to recombine any which way with different dispositions. For now, then, we will use 'quidditism' to refer to the conjunction of I-quidditism and R-quidditism. (For further discussion of varieties of quidditism see Hildebrand 2016; Locke 2012; and Smith 2016).

Lewis (2009) draws a sceptical conclusion from his discussion of quidditism; since all we can ever have epistemic access to is what properties dispose their bearers to *do* in various circumstances, and since knowing a dispositional role is insufficient for knowing which property confers that dispositional role because properties can switch dispositional roles with no detectable difference (as per R-quidditism), we are irremediably ignorant of the *properties in themselves*. Lewis embraces this conclusion, quipping that no one ever promised him that he was capable, in principle, of knowing everything. (Schaffer (2005) argues that Lewis gets the epistemology wrong and that we can, in fact, know the quiddistic natures of properties.)

Others have seen the irremediable ignorance ushered by quidditism as cause for concern.[46] By highlighting the possibility that multiple properties confer the exact same dispositions (something that Schaffer (2005) does not consider), Bird (2007b, 77–8) presents an even more worrisome sceptical implication of quidditism. Given quidditism, it is possible, for example, that two or more properties confer all and only those dispositions that we associate with the *term* 'mass'. We cannot know if such a possibility is indeed realised in our world because there would be no detectable difference between a world in which just one property plays the mass role and a world in which multiple distinct properties play the mass role. A plausible conception of mass as *the* property with such and such a dispositional profile would be undermined if *two or more* properties played the mass role. And since we cannot know whether or not two or more properties occupy the mass role, we cannot know whether this conception of *mass* is undermined. Furthermore, if, as again seems plausible, we *fix the reference* of the term 'mass' via the definite description '*the* property that plays the mass role', then the possibility that ours is a world in which multiple

---

[46] It is worth noting that this consideration arguably only motivates one of the powers theories to be explored here, namely, dispositional essentialism; see subsection 3.5.2 below.

properties play the mass role means that we cannot know if our term 'mass' determinately refers to anything at all. These considerations, according to Bird (2007b, 77), do 'serious damage to our concept of a property', hence he thinks we should reject quidditism (Bird 2007b, 78).

Furthermore, *physics* does not seem to recognise such things as quiddities, that is, properties which are thoroughly independent of their modal profiles. This brings a certain irony given that Lewis's touted motivation for Humeanism was to 'resist philosophical arguments that there are more things in heaven and earth than physics has dreamt of' (Lewis 1994, 474). Demarest (2017, 48), following Cartwright (1999), argues that scientists look for 'dispositional essences, or what it is that things *do* in different situations'. This kind of argument, according to which all of the properties that science tells us about are *essentially* dispositional, has been particularly influential in the debate between quidditists and their opponents (see, e.g., Blackburn 1990, 63; Ellis and Lierse 1994, 32; Harre and Madden 1975; Mckitrick 2003; Mumford 2006; Williams 2011). Why, as Hawthorne puts it, 'posit from the armchair distinctions that are never needed by science?' (Hawthorne 2002, 369).

It is for these kinds of reasons that philosophers have rejected quidditism in favour of the view according to which the dispositions that properties confer are of the *essences* of those properties. Scientifically redundant quiddities are ousted from our ontology and sceptical worries are avoided; to know what dispositions a property confers is to know the essential nature of that property and it is no longer possible that properties swapped dispositional roles or that multiple distinct properties played the very same dispositional role.

Thus, we arrive at a reason for thinking that properties and dispositions are necessarily connected. In the interest of avoiding scepticism and a science-unfriendly ontology, it is maintained that *dispositions constitute the essences of properties* and hence that the identity of a property is not primitive, as per quidditism, but is given in terms of its dispositional relations to other properties. This, in turn, gives rise to necessary connections between properties and dispositions and (according to some) between individual property instances conditional upon the properties they instantiate.

Not everyone is convinced by the sceptical concerns (e.g., Schaffer 2005) nor by the considerations from scientific practice (Locke 2012; Psillos 2006b; Williams 2011) that purport to tell against quidditism. Perhaps, however, one should be less concerned with sceptical arguments and more concerned with the thought that the rejection of quidditism is a natural way to admit irreducible modality in the world, which can then be put to work in a variety of interesting and useful ways.

A more robust motivation for denying quidditism may arise given the conjunction of whatever plausibility the above considerations against quidditism have with the theoretical utility that results from embracing necessary connections between properties and dispositions. The remainder of this section will thus be primarily concerned with the kind of positive argument for powers which says that we should accept the existence of powers because doing so yields a fruitful resource for explaining other phenomena of philosophical interest – our particular focus will be on explaining laws of nature and modality.

3.3.2 Laws of Nature

Arguably, the default approach for powers theorists in thinking about how powers explain laws is that given by *dispositional essentialism*. Dispositional essentialists, such as Ellis (2001), Bird (2007b), and Chakravartty (2003a, 2007) defend the idea that properties are essentially dispositional on the grounds that doing so yields an attractive account of the laws of nature.[47] Laws, according to the dispositional essentialist, 'flow from the essences of properties' (Bird 2007b, 5). Bird makes this idea quite precise, so let's first look at his dispositional essentialist account of the laws of nature.

Bird first notes the connection between dispositionality and counterfactuals. The Simple Conditional Analysis of dispositions says that for x to possess *the disposition to yield manifestation M in response to stimulus S* (let's denote this '$D_{(S, M)}$'), is for x to be such that if it *were* S then it *would* be M:

CA. $D_{(S, M)}x \leftrightarrow (Sx \,\square\!\!\rightarrow Mx)$

We've seen (in Section 2) that there are plenty of issues with this biconditional. However, Bird (2007b, 60–3) provides various arguments to support the idea that it will hold for fundamental dispositions. Moreover, Bird does not endorse CA as an analysis of dispositions. Rather, he takes CA as a necessary equivalence between dispositions and conditionals (Bird 2007b, 43), which he writes as:

CA$\square$. $\square (D_{(S, M)}x \leftrightarrow (Sx \,\square\!\!\rightarrow Mx))$

'Essentially dispositional properties are ones that have the same dispositional character in all possible worlds; that character is the property's *real* rather than

---

[47] Mumford (2004) agrees that there is nothing more to being a property (he eschews essence talk) than the dispositional relations in which it stands to other properties and that this can serve to explain what goes on in the universe, but he maintains that this view of properties obviates the need for laws of nature. For criticisms of Mumford on this score see, e.g., Bird 2007b, ch. 9; Kistler 2020, 171–88.

merely nominal essence' (Bird 2007b, 44). So, from the claim that P has a dispositional essence, Bird infers that for any world, w, and individual, x, such that x instantiates P at w, x will be disposed to yield manifestation M in response to stimulus S (Bird 2007b, 45):

$DE_p.$ $\Box\,(Px \rightarrow D_{(S,\ M)}x)$

Combining CA $\Box$ and DE_p by substituting $D_{(S,\ M)}x$ in DE_p for $(Sx \Box \rightarrow Mx)$ then gives us:

(I) $\Box\,(Px \rightarrow (Sx\ \Box \rightarrow Mx))$

Where (I) says that, necessarily, if x instantiates P, x would yield manifestation M if it were to acquire stimulus S. Now assume (for conditional proof) that x instantiates P and acquires stimulus S:

(II) $Px\ \&\ Sx$

From (I) and (II), and with modus ponens for the counterfactual, we can derive:

(III) Mx

It then follows, by conditional proof, from the assumption in (II) that:

(IV) $(Px\ \&\ Sx) \rightarrow Mx$

And finally, since x is arbitrary, we can generalise, producing:

(V) $\forall x((Px\ \&\ Sx) \rightarrow Mx)$

(V) Is a universal generalisation derived from a statement about the dispositional essence of potency. Furthermore, since the reasoning (I) through to (V) holds in an arbitrary world, (V) is *necessary*:

(V$\Box$) $\Box\forall x((Px\ \&\ Sx) \rightarrow Mx).$

'Hence we have explained the truth of a generalization on the basis of the dispositional essence of a property. This is the core of the dispositional essentialist explanation of laws. Since the generalization is non-accidental it is a nomic generalization' (Bird 2007b, 46).[48]

---

[48] One might worry that the generalisations entailed surely cannot be *universal* since they will only hold *ceteris paribus* at best since the dispositions from which they derive will always be subject to interfering circumstances (see, e.g., Kistler 2010). However, Bird argues that the *fundamental* dispositions from which laws derive will plausibly not be subject to these interferers (finks or masks) (Bird 2007b, 62–3). And the fact that non-fundamental dispositions *are* subject to finks, masks, etc. yields a good explanation of the *ceteris paribus* nature of non-fundamental laws (Bird 2007b, 62–3).

The crucial point here is just that the dispositional essentialist derivation of a law requires that dispositions are constitutive of property essences. As Bird says, this is the *core* of the view. But there is more to be said about what, exactly, the laws *are* on this account: are they universal generalisations, dispositional relationships, or something else? We return to this question in Section 3.5 when we consider whether dispositional essentialism really satisfies its explanatory aims.

Dispositional essentialists claim various benefits for an account of laws as just outlined, such as the modal robustness and explanatory power of laws so conceived. Dispositional essentialism stands in opposition to contingentist accounts of laws, such as the Humean best-system analysis (e.g., Lewis 1983; Loewer 2007), and the nomic necessitation view (Armstrong 1983; Dretske 1977; Tooley 1977). By rendering the laws necessary, dispositional essentialism is able to account for the counterfactual robustness of laws and hence their importance to our scientific and practical endeavours (see also Kimpton-Nye 2020); in order to make predictions and manipulate our environment we need to know which generalisations will continue to hold in different possible scenarios (though see Beebee 2011 for a sceptical response). And the laws are said to possess metaphysical 'oomph', they are metaphysically responsible for property distributions throughout spacetime (on this, dispositional essentialism is in agreement with the nomic necessitation view in opposition to the *descriptive* Humean best-system view of laws).

Dispositional essentialism is not the only powers-based account of laws. Recently, there has been a fair amount of interest in understanding laws as efficient descriptions of how properties are *possibly* distributed throughout spacetime (Demarest 2017; Katzav 2005, 339–40; Kimpton-Nye 2017, 2021b, 2022b; Williams 2019). The properties in question metaphysically explain how they are possibly distributed throughout spacetime by metaphysically explaining the dispositions that they confer upon their bearers; hence the properties explain the laws that describe these possible distributions. Call this view *The Powers–BSA* (because it combines an ontology of powers with a modalised version of Lewis's *best-system analysis* of laws). The Powers–BSA depends on there being necessary connections between properties and dispositions to get its explanatory aspirations off the ground. But contra dispositional essentialism, this powers-based account of the laws of nature does not stipulate that properties have a dispositional essence; it leaves open that the necessary connections between properties and dispositions come about in some other way (more on this in Sections 3.4 and 3.5, see also Kimpton-Nye 2021b).

3.3.3 Modality

Various articulations of 'dispositionalism' about modality invoke the idea that dispositions are connected with possibilities, either via a link with counterfactuals (Borghini and Williams 2008; Jacobs 2010) or directly (Vetter 2015): if x is disposed to φ, then it is possible that φ. Since the connection between dispositions and possibility is conceptual,[49] this is something that even the Humean quidditist can agree with.

What is distinctive of dispositionalism is that it is the properties, viz. *powers*, of *concrete*, *actual* individuals that metaphysically explain these dispositions and, hence, metaphysically explain at least some forms of modality (assume that 'explanation' here is metaphysical).

Consider, for example, a vase, v, which is disposed to break; hence it is possible that v breaks. What explains this disposition and associated modality, according to dispositionalism is a power, or some powers, of the vase. Plausibly, v's disposition to break can ultimately be explained in terms of certain low-level powers such as *mass*, *spin*, and so on. So, it will be these low-level powers that ultimately explain the *possibility* that v breaks, via the dispositions that they explain.

For Lewis (1973b, 1986, 1997), by contrast, it is facts about other possible worlds that ultimately explain the modality associated with dispositions.[50] Dispositionalism does not 'outsource' modality to other possible worlds, it roots modality in the powers of concrete individuals in *this* world (Vetter 2011b). In other words, modality is not reduced to or explained in terms of anything non-modal, it is dispositional properties 'all the way down' (Vetter 2021).[51]

If the connection between properties and dispositions were thoroughly contingent, as per quidditism, then even granting the (conceptual) link between dispositions and possibility, properties themselves would not suffice to explain the corresponding possibilities. For the quidditist, v's instantiating certain low-level properties need not be accompanied by v's being disposed to break – it is metaphysically possible that the properties and the disposition come apart – and hence v's instantiating these properties does not explain the possibility that v breaks. To explain the possibility that v breaks, the quidditist must appeal to

---

[49] Though for a dissenting view, see Jenkins and Nolan 2012.

[50] Lewis analyses dispositions in terms of counterfactual conditionals and then analyses counterfactuals in terms of possible worlds. See also Section 2.

[51] There is a debate about the formal adequacy (can dispositionalism validate the appropriate logical axioms?) and extensional correctness (can dispositionalism account for all of the possibilities that we intuitively think there are?) of modal dispositionalism as an account of metaphysical modality (see, e.g., Kimpton-Nye 2018, 2021; Wang 2015; Yates 2015).

more than just v's physical properties. In general, the quidditist must fill the gap between instantiating some property or properties and being disposed to φ; hence Lewis's appeal to possible worlds and Armstrong's appeal to governing laws. Dispositionalists close this gap by positing explanatory necessary connections between properties and dispositions.

3.3.4 Summing Up

In general terms, then, concerns about property identity and scepticism motivate some to say that property essences are constituted by dispositions and hence to maintain that properties and dispositions are necessarily connected. Positing necessary connections between properties and dispositions is also a necessary condition on *explaining* laws of nature and modality in terms of those properties via an explanation of dispositions, as fans of powers would like to do.

So far, we've discussed the motivation for understanding properties as necessarily connected with dispositions (a minimal necessary condition on a property being a power). The next two sections (3.4 and 3.5) will be concerned with what specific metaphysical account of these necessary connections is apt if properties are to successfully explain laws and modality. As mentioned at the end of Section 3.3.1, there is considerable disagreement, including among advocates of powers (cf. Williams 2011), about how compelling the considerations from property identity, scepticism, and science-friendliness are in motivating powers. For this reason, and due to limitations on space, we will focus primarily on the issues of explaining laws and modality.

3.4 Two Views of the Metaphysics of Powers

In the literature on powers, there is a close connection between the account given of the necessary connections between properties and dispositions and the account of *what it is to be a power* (see, in particular, Tugby 2021). We will outline two such accounts.

The *dispositional essentialist* account of the necessary connections between properties and dispositions is, unsurprisingly, an *essentialist* account. This was discussed above but it bears repeating because is arguably the main view of powers; our aim here is to be more explicit about how necessary connections arise and what this implies about what it is to be a power, according to dispositional essentialism. On this view, dispositions are constitutive of property essences and what it is to be a *power* is to be a property whose essence is exhaustively constituted by dispositions. As Bird puts it 'the essence or identity of a power is determined by its dispositional character' (Bird 2016, 356) (see also, e.g., Chakravartty 2003a; Mumford 2004, respectively, on the idea that powers are what they are in virtue of, or are nothing more than, dispositional relations to other properties). Essence *implies* necessity. If A is part of the essence of X, then there is a necessary connection between X and A: necessarily, if X exists then A exists. For example, if a disposition to warp spacetime is part of the essence of *mass* then there is a necessary connection between *mass* and a disposition to warp spacetime; necessarily, anything that instantiates mass will be disposed to warp spacetime.

Furthermore, what Bird means when he says that properties are essentially dispositional is not *merely* that there is some explanatory necessary connection between property and disposition: the presence of a necessary connection between property and disposition does not suffice for the former to be essentially dispositional and hence does not suffice for a property to be a *power*. Bird thus subscribes to the Finean notion of essence whereby essence *explains*, and hence suffices for, necessity, but not vice versa (Fine 1994), and Bird uses this notion of essence to give an account of what it is to be a power and to account for the necessary connections between properties and dispositions.[52]

> *DE Powers*: to be a power is to be a property whose essence is exhaustively constituted by dispositional relations to other properties[53] (e.g., Bird 2007, 2016, 2018; Chakravartty 2003a; 2007; Mumford 2004).

> *DE Necessity*: powers are necessarily connected with dispositions because dispositions constitute the essences of powers (cf. Fine 1994).

Earlier citations notwithstanding, a recent paper by Mumford suggests that he disagrees with Bird about what suffices for a property to count as a *power*. Mumford (2021) provides numerous examples of properties, of which we may say that their essences can be specified non-dispositionally (such as *sphericity*: to be a sphere is to have a surface, all points on which are equidistant from its centre) but which he nonetheless counts as powers because he thinks that the properties in question are necessarily connected with dispositions. This gives the impression, at least, that Mumford is endorsing a view according to which it *suffices* for a property, P, to be a power that P is necessarily connected with some disposition, D.

Whether or not Mumford really thinks that the presence of a necessary connection between a property and a disposition suffices for that property to count as a power is unclear, since in the aforementioned recent paper he also emphasises the importance of the *dynamic, productive* nature of powers

---

[52] Hence, for example, the dispositions associated with triangularity according to Mellor (1974, 1982) do not suffice for triangularity to count as a *power*, on Bird's view.

[53] According to dispositional essentialism, dispositional relations are thus *Bradlean internal* relations between properties (Tugby 2022a, sec. 3.2), where for a relation to be Bradlean its relata must be partly or wholly constituted by their entering into the relation (Barker 2009, 247; Tugby 2022a, 69).

(cf. Groff 2021), and elsewhere he maintains that '[A property is] nothing more than a set of connections to, and causal powers for, other properties' (Mumford 2004, 185), which would seem to ally him more closely with (Birdian) dispositional essentialism. Nevertheless, this raises an interesting issue. If a property is necessarily connected with a disposition but this disposition is not part of the essence of the property, then what else might account for the necessity?

According to *the grounding view* of powers (see, in particular, Coates 2021, 2022; Ingthorsson 2013; Kimpton-Nye 2018a, 2021b; Tugby 2012, 2021, 2022a, 2022b),[54] it is not necessary for a property, P, to be a power that its essence is constituted by dispositions, contra DE. The grounding view maintains that powers are qualitative in the sense that their essences can be specified wholly independently of any dispositions or modal relations to distinct properties. Powers are, then, necessarily connected with dispositions because they are properties that fully *ground* dispositions.[55] Grounding is generally taken to be a worldly relationship of metaphysical explanation that is *necessitating* (Dasgupta 2014; Fine 2015; Trogdon 2013). At least *full* grounding is necessitating; when we talk about grounding we mean full grounding, unless otherwise stated. So, if A grounds B, then A metaphysically explains B and it is metaphysically necessary that if A obtains then B obtains. Paradigm examples include: *being scarlet* grounding *being red* and Socrates grounding {Socrates}. The idea, then, is that powers ground dispositions and this accounts for the necessary connection between the two.[56]

The grounding view thus comprises the following accounts of what it is to be a power and how the necessary connections between powers and dispositions arise:

> *Grounding Powers*: to be a power is to be a property that fully grounds at least one disposition.[57]

---

[54] See also Kistler (2012) and Audi (2012) for early expressions of something close to the grounding view, and, more recently, Azzano (2019, 2020). One might also find seeds of the view in Smith (2016).

[55] Armstrong's view is also sometimes described as one on which categorical properties ground dispositions. But on Armstrong's view, properties only ground dispositions in conjunction with the (contingent) laws of nature. So, on Armstrong's view, the connection between properties and dispositions is contingent. On the grounding view of powers, powers are properties that fully and directly ground dispositions and hence which are metaphysically necessarily connected with those dispositions.

[56] Coates (2021, 8357) says that the grounding is 'at least partial' because powers are responsible for dispositions only in conjunction with certain 'partner powers' (Heil 2003; Ingthorsson 2013; Martin 1997; Yates 2016). The problem with this is that *quiddities* (i.e., paradigm *non*-powers) could be understood as partially grounding dispositions (in conjunction with governing laws if you are an Armstrongian or the spatio-temporal distribution of properties and facts about possible worlds if you are a Lewisian).

[57] According to the grounding view, dispositional relations are thus *Leibnizian internal* relations between properties (Tugby 2022a, sec. 3.2), where for a relation to be Leibnizian is for it to hold in virtue of monadic features of its relata (Barker 2009, 247; Tugby 2022a, 69).

> *Grounding Necessity*: powers are necessarily connected with dispositions because they fully ground dispositions.

It is worth noting at this point that DE and the grounding view are mutually exclusive. If, as per DE, a property, P, has its essence constituted by a disposition, D, then it cannot be the case that P *grounds* D. And if, as per the grounding view, P grounds D, then it cannot be the case that D constitutes the essence of P. The reason for this, roughly speaking, is that grounded entities are less fundamental than their grounds and it cannot be the case that an entity, x, has as part of its essence anything that is *less* fundamental than x itself (for more detail on this point, see, e.g., Jaag 2014; Tugby 2022a, ch. 3).

Some might say that the *powerful qualities view*, aka the *identity* view, of powers is similar in spirit to the grounding view in that it maintains that powers have both a qualitative and a dispositional 'aspect' or 'side' (Heil 2003; Jacobs 2011; Martin 1997, 2007; Martin and Heil 1999). The key difference, however, is that identity theorists also say that the qualitative and the dispositional are *identical*. This view is motivated in large part by the concern that properties whose essences are exhaustively constituted by dispositions, as per DE, possess 'too little actuality' and hence lead to a vicious regress (e.g., Armstrong 1997, 80). By *identifying* dispositionality with qualitativity, the identity theorists hope to avoid regress by ensuring that properties are 'here and now, actual, not merely potential' (Heil 2012, 59).

However, many think that it is incoherent to identify qualitativity and dispositionality because, for example, qualities and dispositions are metaphysically individuated in different ways – the latter, but not the former, are individuated *relationally* (see, e.g., Tugby 2021, sec. 2). There is also an open debate over whether the identity view just collapses back into dispositional essentialism (Giannotti 2021a, 2021b; Taylor 2018, 2022). Given that the grounding view seems to be able to claim these advantages over the identity view while avoiding its drawbacks, and due to limitations of space, we will say no more about powerful qualities/the identity view.

3.5 Explaining Laws and Modality

So, we have two accounts of powers: dispositional essentialism and the grounding view. Of course, there are other views out there, but we must narrow our focus due to limitations of space. We hope that these views at least represent quite different ends on a spectrum between which we might find variations on the identity view theme.

How, then, are we to decide between the two views? We should decide on the basis of which account renders powers best able to do the primary philosophical work for which they were initially invoked, namely, explaining laws and modality. There is lots of other work to which powers have been put (see, e.g., Anjum and Mumford 2018; Jacobs 2017; Mumford and Anjum 2011; Williams 2019). But again, due to limitations of space we must limit our focus somehow and we think that accounting for laws and modality is the most important and promising work for powers.

3.5.1 Dispositional Essentialism

Let's first consider the dispositional essentialist account of laws of nature. We saw, in Section 3.3.2, Bird's canonical dispositional essentialist account of laws (we refer the reader back to Section 3.3.2 for a refresher). But, as mentioned, Bird's derivation left open what, exactly, laws are. To address this caveat, we need to re-examine the dispositional essentialist metaphysics of powers.

Recall that, according to *DE powers*, to be a power is to be a property whose essence is exhaustively constituted by dispositional relations to other properties (e.g., Bird 2007, 2016, 2018; Chakravartty 2003a, 2007; Mumford 2004). A given power, P, disposes its bearers to yield some characteristic manifestation, M, when appropriately stimulated, S. We can say, then, that the properties P, M, and S stand in the stimulus–response relation (SR relation), which is really just a more precise term for 'dispositional relation'.[58] SR relations are modal; in this case the SR relation's obtaining between P, M, and S amounts to its being the case that if an individual, x, instantiating P *were* to acquire S then it *would* M. Since P is a power, according to dispositional essentialism, the essence of P is *exhausted* by the SR relation(s) in which it stands to other properties.[59] Dispositional essentialists of the type just mentioned (e.g., Bird 2007, 2016, 2018; Chakravartty 2003a, 2007; Mumford 2004) maintain that *all* ontic properties are powers (all fundamental properties, in Bird's case). So, the properties M and S to which P is SR related will also have their essences exhaustively constituted by SR relations to other properties and so on. Properties, on this view are nodes in a structure of SR relations and their identities are given by their place in that structure (cf. Bird 2007a).

This is the dispositional essentialist's *structuralist* metaphysics of powers. Bringing this back to our concern with laws of nature, we can now ask: where do laws fit into this picture? Answer: laws are *arcs* in the structure. What's the evidence for this? Both Chakravartty (2003a, 2007) and Bird (2007b) explicitly

---

[58] The idea originates in Bird (2007b), though the 'SR' terminology was coined earlier in Barker and Smart (2012).

[59] To be clear, SR relations are second-order relations and have nothing to do with relations between objects that instantiate these properties: SR relations can hold even if particular instances of P are never stimulated and manifested.

claim that laws of nature are modal *relations* between powers and (as Kimpton-Nye (2021b, 3426) discusses in more detail), since SR relations fit the bill here, it is reasonable to attribute to Chakravartty and to Bird the view that SR relations just are the laws.[60]

> *DE laws 1*: Laws are the dispositional relations that constitute the essences of powers and hence make up the property structure.

This is consistent with the idea that a *statement* of a law (linguistic entity) may derive from a statement of the essence of a property (linguistic entity) in accordance with the derivation presented in Section 3.3.2 (and in Bird 2007b, 43–8). What we have done here, however, is to take a deeper dive into the metaphysics.

The question now is whether the dispositional essentialist picture just presented satisfies its explanatory goals. We will show that there are reasons to think that it does not.

There are two broad explanatory concerns for dispositional essentialism. The first is that powers and laws appear to symmetrically ground each other, which significantly threatens the dispositional essentialist claim to metaphysically explain laws in terms of powers. The second is that dispositional essentialism is subject to an explanatory regress closely analogous to that levelled by Bird (2005) at the Armstrongian view of laws (Armstrong 1983) (see also Dretske 1977; Tooley 1977). We'll address these in turn, before drawing out the implications for explaining modality in terms of dispositional essentialism's structuralist metaphysics of powers.

If properties are identity dependent on their position in a structure, as per the dispositional essentialist picture sketched, then it seems that properties are *grounded* by the structure. The structure, in this case, *is* a structure of SR relations which the dispositional essentialist is plausibly interpreted as identifying with laws of nature. Hence, properties are grounded by *laws*. This alone should set alarm bells ringing since the dispositional essentialist project was originally conceived of as metaphysically explaining laws in terms of properties, not vice versa. But things get worse. The structure itself is plausibly *composed* of properties, at least this is something we should wish to say if we want to avoid commitment to relations without relata (Chakravartty 1998, 2003b; Kimpton-Nye 2021b, 3431; Psillos 2006a); it thus also seems that properties ground the structure (on the plausible assumption that composition

---

[60] Here is Bird's official statement of what the laws are: 'The laws of a domain are the fundamental, general explanatory *relationships* between kinds, quantities, and qualities of that domain, that supervene upon the essential natures of those things' (Bird 2007b, 201, emphasis added); and according to Chakravartty (2007, 150) 'Causal laws are nothing more than relations between casual properties.'

is a grounding relation): properties and structure *symmetrically* ground each other (cf. Godfrey 2020; Kimpton-Nye 2021b; Yates 2018). This would render dispositional essentialism *incoherent* if it were also thought that grounding is an asymmetric relation (though this has been debated; see, e.g., Barnes 2018; Rodriguez-Pereyra 2015; Thompson 2016). (See also Barker 2013; Jaag 2014; Sider 2020, ch. 2; Tugby 2022a, ch. 3 for slightly different presentations of this line of argument.)

At this point one may think that the best response is to reject the identification of laws with SR relations, where the latter, remember, are arcs in the property structure, i.e., ontic as opposed to linguistic entities. If laws were instead conceived of *linguistically* as universal generalisations (such as 'all Fs are Gs') then it could be maintained that properties with their essences constituted by SR relations (i.e., *powers*) *explain* or *make true* the laws (qua linguistic entities), and this would remain in keeping with the dispositional essentialist spirit. But since no universal generalisation is *identical* with any SR relation (these are just different kinds of entity), even if SR relations ground properties (as above) it no longer follows that *laws* ground properties and the symmetrical grounding worry is blocked. Hence, we get the following:

DE laws 2: laws are universal generalisations that are made true by properties.

How are we to understand the claim that properties *make true* or *explain* universal generalisations? It has been argued (Barker 2013; Barker and Smart 2012) that a structuralist metaphysics of properties cannot meet this explanatory demand. Property essences, according to the structuralist dispositional essentialist, are exhausted by the SR relations in which they stand to other properties. So, if we ask what explains or makes it true that all Fs are Gs, the dispositional essentialist explanation in terms of properties must appeal to the SR relations constitutive of the essences of the properties F and G (see Tugby 2012, 725). So, the explanation goes roughly as follows: 'the fact that F and G enter into such and such an SR relation explains why all Fs are Gs'. But now we may ask why the fact that F and G enter into the SR relation ensures that all Fs are in fact Gs. Is there some higher order relation which ensures that if F and G enter into the SR relation then all Fs are Gs? To go along this route would be to fall into a vicious explanatory regress. In fact, Barker and Smart (2012) argue that dispositional essentialism succumbs to the exact same problem as that raised by Bird (2005) against Armstrong's (1983) view of laws. Both dispositional essentialism and the Armstrongian view seek to explain the distributions of properties in terms of nomic relations between properties. But both views are thus subject to the objection that it is unclear how these relations are supposed to do their explanatory work (why couldn't F and G enter into the SR relation and there be an F that is not G?). It would be antagonistic to dispositional essentialism to just repudiate this explanatory demand and maintain that it is just a brute necessity that if F and G enter into the SR relation then all Fs are Gs – because the whole point of dispositional essentialism was to explain property distributions, and, more generally, *laws*, in terms of those property essences rather than in terms of brute necessity (perhaps it is the essence or the 'business' of SR relations that they determine the relevant generalisations (Schaffer 2016b), but this still seems to sacrifice the aim of explaining laws in terms of properties).[61]

Furthermore, the apparent inability of structuralist powers to explain their own distributions means that it would not help to twin this account of powers with The Powers–BSA account of laws as descriptions of *possible* property distributions. This is because, if the Barker and Smart regress argument is taken seriously, structuralist powers are no more capable of explaining their own possible first-order distributions than they are of explaining how they are actually distributed.

This last point is relevant to the project of explaining modality more generally. Another way of conceiving of the dispositional essentialist's explanatory project is as explaining how properties are *possibly* distributed throughout spacetime. It was suggested that dispositional essentialism struggles to explain why it is necessary that if F and G enter into the SR relation, then all Fs are Gs. In other words, dispositional essentialism struggles to explain why it is not *possible* that F-ness and G-ness are distributed such that there is an instance of F at some spatio-temporal location x, y, z, t that is not also an instance of G. Hence, dispositional essentialism struggles to explain the *modal* constraints on individual property bearers. But explaining modal constraints on individuals in terms of the properties that they instantiate is at the heart of a powers-based account of modality.

Another problem for explaining modality is as follows. We said above that a dispositionalist account of modality proceeds by metaphysically explaining dispositional modality in terms of properties of concrete individuals. But if dispositional modality in the form of SR relations constitute the essences of those properties, then it looks like the dispositional modality metaphysically explains the properties because they make them the properties they are by constituting their essences. But if dispositional modality metaphysically explains properties, properties cannot metaphysically explain that same modality, on the assumption that metaphysical explanation (i.e., *grounding*) is asymmetric. This is just the symmetrical grounding worry targeted at the dispositional essentialist who seeks to explain modality via its structuralist powers metaphysic (see also Jaag 2014 and Tugby 2022a, ch. 3).

---

[61] Though see Friend (2022a) for a recent defence of Bird on this score.

3.5.2 The Grounding View

Powers, on this view, are qualities that *ground* dispositions and this is what accounts for the necessary connections between powers and dispositions.

How might the grounding view explain laws of nature? Again, there are at least two options available. One might identify laws with the dispositional relations that powers *ground*; or one might identify laws with regularities in the (possible) distributions of powers:

> *Grounding laws 1*: Laws are the dispositional relations that powers ground.

> *Grounding laws 2*: Laws are regularities in the (possible) distributions of powers.[62]

To opt for *Grounding laws 1* would be to stay closer to dispositional essentialism, according to which laws are dispositional relations in the property structure. But unlike dispositional essentialism, the grounding view does not thus yield an account on which powers and laws symmetrically ground each other because it rejects the idea that the essences of powers are exhaustively constituted by dispositions. If laws are identified with dispositional relations, then, the grounding relation has the desired asymmetry: running from powers to laws and not vice versa. And the fact that different powers ground different dispositions is accounted for by the fact that different powers have different thick qualitative essences.

Alternatively, one could opt for *Grounding laws 2*. Again, the grounding view maintains that properties/powers have thick qualitative essences and that this is what accounts for the different dispositions grounded by different properties. It is thus *not* the case, on this view, that all there is by way of explanation for the possible distributions of properties is dispositional relations between properties; hence the explanatory regress that threatens the dispositional essentialist explanation of property distributions (Barker and Smart 2012) is avoided by the grounding view (as argued by Tugby 2012).

Similarly, if dispositions and hence possible property distributions can be explained by the grounding view, then it is plausible that the grounding view could provide a good property-based account of the metaphysics of modality too.

While the grounding view arguably dodges the explanatory deficiencies of dispositional essentialism, it does face some challenges. Chief among these is

---

[62] Tugby (2022a) proposes something close to *Grounding laws 1*. And Kimpton-Nye (2021b) proposes something close to *Grounding laws 2* (see also Demarest 2017; Kimpton-Nye 2017, though these papers do not concern themselves with the issue of the grounding view versus dispositional essentialism). But it is important to emphasise that these options are by no means intended to be exhaustive.

the following: one may worry that it is not explanatory to merely *stipulate* that properties ground dispositions. And since, for the dispositionalist, explaining dispositions is a prerequisite for explaining laws and modality, the worry is that the grounding view does not outperform DE after all.[63]

Maybe it is explanatory to say that being scarlet grounds being red because it is just a priori that a grounding link obtains between *being scarlet* and *being red*. But it is not a priori that something instantiating *mass* is disposed to warp spacetime (for example), so why think there is a grounding link between property and disposition? In response to this worry, Tugby (2021, 2022b) and Kimpton-Nye (2021b) have taken inspiration from Schaffer (2017) to argue that it is not the case that all grounding links must be the sorts of things that we know a priori. If there are good theoretical reasons to posit a grounding link, we are justified in believing that it exists, even if it is conceivable that it does not exist.

3.6 How Far Does the Powers Ontology Extend?

Powers theorists disagree about the extent of the powers ontology. Are all properties powers? Are most? Are only a select few? This subsection will explore what the different accounts of powers discussed – dispositional essentialism and the grounding view – imply about which properties get to count as powers.[64]

3.6.1 Bird's Conservative View

Alexander Bird (2016, 2018) addresses the question of which properties get to count as powers and argues that only fundamental properties and some evolved macro (i.e., non-fundamental) properties are powers. Central to Bird's argument is his dispositional essentialist conception of the metaphysics of powers according to which a power is an ontic (as opposed to a merely predicatory) property whose essence/identity is given purely dispositionally (e.g., Bird 2016, 246, 2018, 248, 249). As discussed above, an important consequence of this metaphysics of powers is what Bird calls 'modal fixity'.

---

[63] Another worry is that since, on the grounding view, property essences are not exhaustively constituted by dispositions, the grounding view cannot rule out the possibility that one and the same disposition is grounded by different properties in different instances in the same world and hence the sceptical worries come back to bite. But, as mentioned, there is not much consensus on how worrisome we should really take these epistemological/semantic issues to be. Indeed, one may just maintain that such issues are distinct from and can have no critical bearing on the properly *metaphysical* issues with which the powers metaphysic is primarily concerned.

[64] This subsection draws upon and contains some material from article, 'Pandispositionalism and the metaphysics of powers' (Kimpton-Nye 2022a), published open access in *Synthese* under a Creative Commons Attribution 4.0 International License.

Modal Fixity: Powers are modally fixed properties (have invariant [dispositional] characters across possible worlds) (Bird 2018, 249).

In other words: powers are necessarily connected with dispositions.

As we have seen, powers have been put to fruitful work explaining laws of nature, modality, and property identity. Laws and modality are explained via an explanation of the actual and possible pattern of property instances throughout spacetime. And, Bird, e.g., maintains that the dispositional essentialist account of powers yields an account of property identity that is superior to quidditism in that it avoids scepticism and achieves a degree of continuity with science.

Now while these arguments for powers (see Section 3.3 for details) may count in favour of the existence of fundamental properties being powers, Bird argues that they do not support the existence of macro powers. In the case of laws, perhaps we can mount a case for the existence of fundamental powers on the basis of their ability to explain fundamental laws. But we do not also need macro powers to explain non-fundamental laws because, according to Bird, non-fundamental laws supervene on fundamental laws and so are ultimately explained by *fundamental powers*. Similarly for modality, possibilities for things with macro properties need not be explained in terms of macro powers since 'what is possible or not regarding things with non-fundamental properties supervenes on what is possible or not regarding things with fundamental properties' (Bird 2018, 251). And while it is plausible that only quidditism or the powers view may account for the identity of fundamental properties, macro properties may be accounted for in terms of composition or structure (Bird 2018, 251). So, rejection of quidditism does not force one to accept the powers view of property identity for macro properties.

Bird also offers some direct counterexamples to pandispositionalism: i.e., properties in science which concern structure, composition, or relations as opposed to *disposition* (Bird 2016, 355). Examples, from chemistry, biology, and medicine, respectively, include: *being covalent* (of a bond, in virtue of the electron distribution giving rise to the bond), *being heterozygous at a particular locus* (having different alleles at that locus), and *being pericardial* (the property of surrounding the heart) (Bird 2016, 355).

Perhaps the pandispositionalist could respond that the above properties are nonetheless invariably associated with certain dispositions. Mumford (2021) pursues this line with respect to *sphericity*, in response to Bird's critique of macro powers. But this misses Bird's point: even if sphericity were necessarily connected with certain dispositions, this would not suffice for it to count as a power, according to Bird, because the essence and identity of sphericity is not given by its dispositions but by non-dispositional mathematical/structural features. Another example explicitly discussed by Bird is *aromaticity*: even if there were some set of dispositions shared by all aromatic compounds, Bird argues that *aromaticity* would not satisfy his definition of a power, since these dispositions would not determine the essence, nature, or identity of *aromaticity* because 'what aromaticity *is* is a matter of the structure of the molecules and their bonds and electrons' (Bird 2016, 356). While this shared structure may *explain* the fact that aromatic compounds share some set of dispositions, any *necessary connection* between aromaticity and dispositions does not imply a relationship of essence (Bird 2016, 356) (as per Fine 1994).

More recently, Bird (2018) has argued that some *evolved* macro properties *are* powers. He considers the example of *sightedness*. Sightedness is selected because having sight confers an evolutionary advantage on animals. So, the presence of sightedness can be given an evolutionary *explanation*. Sightedness is also itself *explanatory* of other phenomena. Sightedness explains how animals find what they need in their environment and it can explain the appearance of prey animals that camouflage, such as the stick insect. The explanatory role of sightedness is good evidence that it is a real property in the world as opposed to a mere linguistic entity (Bird 2018, 256–7). What's more, sightedness is multiply realisable and so not reducible to more fundamental properties and is explanatory in a way that its realisers in any instance are not. Bird thus argues that the *essence* of sightedness can only be given in terms of how it disposes its bearers and hence that sightedness is a power (Bird 2018, 257–61).

Sightedness is just an example to illustrate the broader point: any evolved, functional, non-fundamental property will be a macro power, according to Bird (though see Vetter's (2018) response according to which Bird's argument for macro powers actually opens the door to far more macro powers than intended).

If one endorses dispositional essentialism, then, one may be inclined to be somewhat restrictive about which properties get to count as powers: if we are convinced by Bird's arguments, only the fundamental properties and some evolved macro properties are powers.

3.6.2 Grounding Pandispositionalism?

Bird's arguments for a restricted ontology of powers depend on his claim that to be a power a property must have its essence exhaustively constituted by dispositions. The grounding view denies that the essences of powers are constituted by dispositions and maintains that powers are properties with qualitative essences that *ground* dispositions. What, then, does the grounding view imply about the extent of the powers ontology? We will argue that it yields the result that *all* properties are powers, i.e., it implies the truth of *pandispositionalism*.

What's more, this is non-trivial because there is also good independent reason to believe that there are a great many ontic *macro* properties in non-fundamental science. Indeed, these are the same sorts of reasons that Bird himself appeals to, as mentioned above: many macro properties play crucial explanatory roles in science and are multiply realisable and so cannot plausibly be eliminated or reduced to the fundamental properties.

First of all, it is worth noting that the grounding view of powers renders Bird's direct argument against pandispositionalism, the argument that appealed to counterexamples, unsound. According to the grounding view, it is no obstacle to a property being a power that its essence can be specified structurally, compositionally, or, more generally, independently of any dispositional relations to other properties. Hence, there is nothing to prevent the properties that Bird cites as 'counterexamples' to pandispositionalism from being powers after all.

But given the grounding view there are also positive reasons for endorsing a great many macro powers and even pandispositionalism. It helps to work with an example here. *Aromaticity* is a chemical property that Bird discusses and takes to be a counterexample to pandispositionalism. But although Bird denies that aromaticity is a power (because it has a qualitative essence), he remains open to its being the case that aromaticity explains dispositions of its bearers and that aromaticity is necessarily connected with these dispositions. Evidence for this is in the following passage:

> Even if we can light on a set of dispositions shared (necessarily) by all aromatic compounds, that complex of dispositions would neither be nor determine the nature, essence or identity of aromaticity. Rather, what aromaticity *is* is a matter of the structure of the molecules and their bonds and electrons. That in turn *explains* any shared dispositions. The necessity of any relationship between aromaticity and a disposition does not amount to a relationship of essence (or nature or identity). (Bird 2016, 356)

It seems, then, that Bird is happy to admit that qualitative properties, such as aromaticity, can explain dispositions and that they are necessarily connected with those dispositions.

From the assumption that aromaticity explains a disposition, and with sufficient *anti-Humean sympathies* not to want to deny necessary connections between properties and the dispositions they explain, it can be argued that aromaticity *grounds* that disposition and hence that aromaticity is a power according to the grounding view of powers.

To see why this is so, consider first that explanations are generally thought to receive *support* from somewhere: paradigmatically, *causal* relations. The breaking of the window is explained by my throwing the stone and this explanation is supported by the causal relation between the stone throwing and the window breaking. But recently, the idea of non-causal explanation has become increasingly mainstream. Now granting that aromaticity explains a disposition to produce aromatic ring currents (for example),[65] one may wonder what supports *this* explanation? Causation doesn't fit the bill here. Aromaticity arguably doesn't *cause* a disposition to produce aromatic ring currents since the two properties vary *synchronically* with one another. The instant aromaticity is present so is the disposition to produce aromatic ring currents but causal relations are generally thought to be *diachronic* (see, e.g., Craver 2007; Kim 2000; Mellor 1995; Russell 1912; and Friend 2019 for a reply) .

What seems more likely is that the relation between aromaticity and a disposition to produce aromatic ring currents is a grounding relation (see, e.g., Schaffer 2016a and Wilson 2018 for a relevant discussion of the similarities between grounding and causation and the associated kinds of explanation). Furthermore, we don't want to say that instead of aromaticity grounding the disposition to produce aromatic ring currents this disposition *constitutes the essence of* aromaticity. This just seems implausible for the sorts of reasons that Bird highlights, i.e., the essence of aromaticity is compositional/ structural, not dispositional. What's more (as discussed in subsection 3.5.1) if the essence of aromaticity were *constituted* by the disposition to produce aromatic ring currents, it seems that aromaticity would thereby be rendered incapable of explaining that disposition (cf. Jaag 2014; Kimpton-Nye 2021b), and to deny aromaticity this explanatory role would be odd indeed. Given that aromaticity explains a disposition to produce aromatic ring currents, then, there are good reasons to believe that aromaticity *grounds* this disposition (again, assuming, that is, broadly anti-Humean sympathies such that one does not balk at the necessity induced by grounding). In conjunction with the grounding view of powers, it follows that aromaticity is a power. Furthermore, understanding the relationship between power and disposition as a *grounding* relationship accounts for *Modal Fixity* and, relatedly, the fact that properties do *not* freely recombine, which is distinctive of the powers metaphysic (see Tugby 2021, sec. 5) for discussion of the relation between grounding theories of powers and (anti)Humeanism).

At this point, a reductionist might object that aromaticity does not explain a disposition to produce aromatic ring currents because all the explanatory work

---

[65] Aromatic ring currents: Delocalised π electrons in the aromatic ring are free to circulate. An electric current can thus be induced if a magnetic field is directed perpendicular to the plane of the aromatic system (as a result of Ampère's law). The ring current then generates a magnetic field inside the aromatic ring that is in the opposite direction to the external magnetic field that induces the current.

is ultimately done by the fundamental properties, charge, spin, mass, etc. to which aromaticity *reduces*. But many take this sort of strong reductionism to be implausible. Among the anti-reductionists is, presumably, Bird himself given that he explicitly cites aromaticity as an example of a macro ontic property (that he thinks is not a power). Schaffer voices a similar anti-reductionist sentiment regarding the property of being a synapse: 'Being a synapse, for instance, involves possessing the power to transmit a pulse from one neuron to another. No fundamental property has this power' (Schaffer 2004, 95). And Schaffer finds support for this kind of anti-reductionism in Kim: 'Having a mass of 1 kilogram has causal powers that no smaller masses have, and water molecules, or the property of being water, have causal powers not had by individual hydrogen or oxygen atoms' (Kim 1998, 108). Now if we read 'having a (causal) power' as 'explaining a disposition',[66] then the point is just that something similar is plausibly maintained regarding aromaticity: the dispositions that aromaticity explains really are not to be explained instead by the fundamental properties and hence it really is aromaticity doing the explaining.

The debate about reductionism is of course far deeper than we have space to do justice to here. But hopefully it can be seen that there is at least some plausibility to the idea that the type of reductionism required to deny that macro properties explain dispositions can be resisted, and hence that there is some reason to think that there are macro *powers*, given the grounding view. It would also be beyond our scope to pre-empt and respond to other objections at this point; for further such attempts see Kimpton-Nye (2022a).

The argument of this subsection so far has focused on the example of aromaticity (though the Schaffer and Kim quotes suggest that it can plausibly be extended to *being a synapse, having mass 1 kg,* and *being water*). But as far as the argument is concerned, there is nothing special about aromaticity. There is reason to think that the argument is sufficiently general to imply that *all* ontic properties are powers.

On the assumption that pandispositionalism is false, there must be at least one (ontic) property that is not a power. What this means, on the grounding view, is that there is at least one property that does not ground *any* dispositions. But being both an ontic property and not grounding any dispositions is a very difficult conjunction for an entity to satisfy.

---

[66] As mentioned in Sections 1 and 3.1, 'power' and 'disposition' are often used interchangeably in the literature, but part of our aim in this Element is to distinguish these notions such that powers might be understood as ontic properties which explain dispositions; hence this reading is appropriate in the current context.

Plausibly, for a property to be *ontic* it must be the case that it explains at least one disposition, i.e., a property couldn't claim to be ontic if it didn't explain any dispositions. Bird himself seems to endorse this idea (Bird 2016, 357, 2018, 258–9), which is also echoed in Schaffer (2004) and Kim (1998), cited above. This also chimes with the spirit of Armstrong's *Eleatic Principle*, roughly according to which contributing to the causal order of the world is the mark of the *real* (see, e.g., Armstrong 1978, 2004; Heil 2003). The first premise of the general argument, then, is:

For all X, if X is an ontic property, then X explains some dispositions of its bearers.

It was argued above that what *supports* the explanatory relation between property and disposition, according to the powers theorist who endorses the grounding view, is *grounding*. So, granting that a given property, P, is ontic and, hence, that P explains dispositions, it will follow that P grounds the dispositions that it explains. The second premise of the argument is thus:

For all X, if X explains some dispositions, then X grounds those dispositions.

The third premise is just a statement of the grounding view:

For all X, if X grounds some dispositions, then X is a power.

Pandispositionalism follows from these three premises:

P1: For all X, if X is an ontic property, then X explains some dispositions of its bearers. (This gains support from Bird (2016, 2018) as well as Schaffer's *scientific conception* of sparse/ontic properties (Schaffer 2004); see also Armstrong's Eleatic Principle (Armstrong 1978, 2004; Heil 2003).)

P2: For all X, if X explains some dispositions, then X grounds those dispositions. (From sympathy to powers and the argument in subsection 3.6.2)

P3: For all X, if X grounds some dispositions, then X is a power. (From the grounding view of powers.)

Conclusion: For all X, if X is an ontic property, then X is a power, i.e., pandispositionalism is true.

In order to resist pandispositionalism, then, one must refute one of P1–P3 in the argument. An argument for P2 has been presented above. Refutation of P1 would require significant argument. To refute P1 in the service of denying pandispositionalism, one would have to provide *at least one* example of a property that is both ontic and which does not explain any dispositions. But finding even one example of an ontic property that does not explain any dispositions is an incredibly tall order. This is because a property, P's, failing to be explanatory in this way would appear to be the mark of P's not contributing to the causal order of the world and hence not being 'real'. Or, put another way, P's failing to be explanatory in this way would seem to tell in favour of P's being eliminable in favour of/reducible to some more fundamental and genuinely explanatory properties (see, e.g., Bird 2018, 258–9), and hence of P's *not* being a genuine constituent of our ontology. P3 is just the assumption that the grounding view is true; we discussed why one might endorse this in subsection 3.5.2, though of course we recognise that further objections to the grounding view may come to light. We thus conclude that *if* the grounding view is true, then *all ontic properties are powers*, i.e., pandispositionalism is true.

3.7 Summary

This Section discussed the metaphysics of powers and the explanatory philosophical work to which powers are put. It was argued that it is a necessary condition on a property, P's, being a power that P is necessarily connected with at least one disposition, D. This raises the question of how necessary connections between powers and dispositions arise. We explored some answers to this question, which was tantamount to exploring the metaphysics of powers, i.e., exploring *what it is* for a property, P, to be a power. Of the two options discussed, dispositional essentialism and the grounding view, the grounding view offered hope of overcoming certain influential critiques of the project of explaining laws and modality in terms of powers. We then asked: which properties count as powers? It was argued that the answer to this question depends on the metaphysics of powers. Dispositional essentialism yields a more conservative answer: just fundamental properties and some evolved macro properties are powers. The grounding view, by contrast, seems to yield the result that *all* properties are powers. The broad moral, then, is that there is a family of interrelated issues concerning powers. Questions about the metaphysics of powers, the explanatory work of powers, and the extent of the powers ontology cannot be considered in isolation from each other.

References

Aimar, Simona. 2019. 'Disposition Ascriptions'. *Philosophical Studies* 176 (7): 1667–92. https://doi.org/10.1007/s11098-018-1084-9.

Anjum, Rani Lill, and Stephen Mumford. 2018. *What Tends to Be: The Philosophy of Dispositional Modality.* 1st ed. Routledge.

Armstrong, David Malet. 1978. *Universals and Scientific Realism.* Cambridge University Press.

1983. *What Is a Law of Nature?* Cambridge University Press.

1997. *A World of States of Affairs.* Cambridge University Press.

2004. *Truth and Truthmakers.* Cambridge University Press.

Audi, Paul. 2012. 'A Clarification and Defense of the Notion of Grounding'. In *Metaphysical Grounding: Understanding the Structure of Reality*, edited by Benjamin Schnieder and Fabrice Correia, 101–21. Cambridge University Press. https://doi.org/10.1017/CBO9781139149136.004.

Azzano, Lorenzo. 2019. 'The Question of Realism for Powers'. *Synthese* 196 (1): 329–54. https://doi.org/10.1007/s11229-017-1478-9.

2020. 'Dispositionality, Categoricity, and Where to Find Them'. *Synthese* 199 (1–2): 2949–76. https://doi.org/10.1007/s11229-020-02917-4.

Backmann, Marius. 2018. 'No Time for Powers'. *Inquiry* 62 (May): 1–29. https://doi.org/10.1080/0020174X.2018.1470569.

Barker, Stephen. 2009. 'Dispositional Monism, Relational Constitution and Quiddities'. *Analysis* 69 (2): 242–50. https://doi.org/10.1093/analys/anp009.

2013. 'The Emperor's New Metaphysics of Powers'. *Mind* 122 (487): 605–53. https://doi.org/10.1093/mind/fzt082.

Barker, Stephen, and Ben Smart. 2012. 'The Ultimate Argument against Dispositional Monist Accounts of Laws'. *Analysis* 72 (4): 714–22. https://doi.org/10.1093/analys/ans114.

Barnes, Elizabeth. 2018. 'Symmetric Dependence'. In *Reality and Its Structure*, edited by Ricki Leigh Bliss and Graham Priest, 50–69. Oxford University Press.

Beebee, Helen. 2011. 'Necessary Connections and the Problem of Induction'. *Noûs* 45 (3): 504–27.

Bird, Alexander. 1998. 'Dispositions and Antidotes'. *Philosophical Quarterly* 48 (191): 227–34. https://doi.org/10.1111/1467-9213.00098.

2005. 'The Ultimate Argument against Armstrong's Contingent Necessitation View of Laws'. *Analysis* 65 (2): 147–55.

2007a. 'The Regress of Pure Powers?' *Philosophical Quarterly (1950–)* 57 (229): 513–34.

2007b. *Nature's Metaphysics: Laws and Properties.* Oxford University Press.

2012. 'Dispositional Expressions'. In *Routledge Companion to the Philosophy of Language*, edited by Gillian Russell and Delia Graff Fara, 729–40. Routledge.

2016. 'Overpowering: How the Powers Ontology Has Overreached Itself'. *Mind* 125 (498): 341–83.

2018. 'I – Fundamental Powers, Evolved Powers, and Mental Powers'. *Aristotelian Society Supplementary Volume* 92 (1): 247–75. https://doi .org/10.1093/arisup/aky006.

2020. 'Possibility and the Analysis of Dispositions'. *Philosophical Inquiries* 8 (1): 83–96. https://doi.org/10.4454/philinq.v8i1.276.

Black, Robert. 2000. 'Against Quidditism'. *Australasian Journal of Philosophy* 78 (1): 87–104. https://doi.org/10.1080/00048400012349371.

Blackburn, Simon. 1990. 'Filling in Space'. *Analysis* 50 (2): 62–65. https://doi .org/10.2307/3328847.

Borghini, Andrea, and Neil E. Williams. 2008. 'A Dispositional Theory of Possibility'. *Dialectica* 62 (1): 21–41. https://doi.org/10.1111/j.1746-8361.2007.01130.x.

Brower, Bruce W. 1993. 'Dispositional Ethical Realism'. *Ethics* 103 (2): 221–49.

Carnap, Rudolf. 1936. 'Testability and Meaning'. *Philosophy of Science* 3 (4): 419–71. https://doi.org/10.1086/286432.

Cartwright, Nancy. 1999. *The Dappled World: A Study of the Boundaries of Science.* Cambridge University Press.

Chakravartty, Anjan. 1998. 'Semirealism'. *Studies in History and Philosophy of Science Part A* 29 (3): 391–408. https://doi.org/10.1016/S0039-3681(98) 00013-2.

2003a. 'The Dispositional Essentialist View of Properties and Laws'. *International Journal of Philosophical Studies* 11 (4): 393–413.

2003b. 'The Structuralist Conception of Objects'. *Philosophy of Science* 70 (5): 867–78. https://doi.org/10.1086/377373.

2007. *A Metaphysics for Scientific Realism: Knowing the Unobservable.* Cambridge University Press.

Chen, Eddy Keming, and Sheldon Goldstein. 2022. 'Governing without a Fundamental Direction of Time: Minimal Primitivism about Laws of Nature'. In *Rethinking the Concept of Law of Nature*, edited by Yemima Ben-Menahem, 21–64. Springer.

Choi, Sungho. 2003. 'Improving Bird's Antidotes'. *Australasian Journal of Philosophy* 81 (4): 573–80. https://doi.org/10.1080/713659764.

2005. 'Dispositions and Mimickers'. *Philosophical Studies* 122: 183–8.

2008. 'Dispositional Properties and Counterfactual Conditionals'. *Mind* 117 (468): 795–841. https://doi.org/10.1093/mind/fzn054.

Coates, Ashley. 2021. 'Making Sense of Powerful Qualities'. *Synthese* 198: 8347–63. https://doi.org/10.1007/s11229-020-02576-5.

2022. 'Tropes, Unmanifested Dispositions and Powerful Qualities'. *Erkenntnis* 87: 2143–60. https://doi.org/10.1007/s10670-020-00295-4.

Constantin, Jan. 2018. 'A Dispositional Account of Practical Knowledge'. *Philosophical Studies* 175 (9): 2309–29. https://doi.org/10.1007/s11098-017-0960-z.

Contessa, Gabriele. 2013. 'Dispositions and Interferences'. *Philosophical Studies* 165 (2): 401–19. https://doi.org/10.1007/s11098-012-9957-9.

2016. 'Dispositions and Tricks'. *Erkenntnis* 81 (3): 587–96. https://doi.org/10.1007/s10670-015-9756-8.

Craver, Carl F. 2007. *Explaining the Brain: Mechanisms and the Mosaic Unity of Neuroscience*. Oxford University Press.

Cross, Troy. 2005. 'What Is a Disposition?' *Synthese* 144 (3): 321–41. https://doi.org/10.1007/s11229-005-5857-2.

Dasgupta, Shamik. 2014. 'On the Plurality of Grounds'. *Philosophers' Imprint* 14: 1–28.

Demarest, Heather. 2017. 'Powerful Properties, Powerless Laws'. In *Causal Powers*, 1st ed., edited by Jonathan Jacobs, 38–53. Oxford University Press.

Donati, Donatella. 2018. 'No Time for Powers'. Ph.D. thesis, University of Nottingham.

Dretske, Fred I. 1977. 'Laws of Nature'. *Philosophy of Science* 44 (2): 248–68.

Ellis, Brian. 2001. *Scientific Essentialism*. Cambridge University Press.

2002. *The Philosophy of Nature: A Guide to the New Essentialism*. 1st ed. Routledge.

Ellis, Brian, and Caroline Lierse. 1994. 'Dispositional Essentialism'. *Australasian Journal of Philosophy* 72 (1): 27–45.

Fara, Michael. 2005. 'Dispositions and Habituals'. *Noûs* 39 (1): 43–82. https://doi.org/10.1111/j.0029-4624.2005.00493.x.

Fine, Kit. 1994. 'Essence and Modality: The Second Philosophical Perspectives Lecture'. *Philosophical Perspectives* 8: 1–16. https://doi.org/10.2307/2214160.

2015. 'Unified Foundations for Essence and Ground'. *Journal of the American Philosophical Association* 1 (2): 296–311. https://doi.org/10.1017/apa.2014.26.

Friebe, Cord. 2018. 'Metaphysics of Laws and Ontology of Time'. *THEORIA: An International Journal for Theory, History and Foundations of Science* 33 (1): 77–89. https://doi.org/10.1387/theoria.17178.

Friend, Toby. 2019. 'Can Parts Cause Their Wholes?' *Synthese* 196 (12): 5061–82. https://doi.org/10.1007/s11229-018-1694-y.

2021. 'Megarian Variable Actualism'. *Synthese* 199 (3–4): 10521–41. https://doi.org/10.1007/s11229-021-03257-7.

2022a. 'Second-Order Relations and Nomic Regularities'. *Philosophical Studies* 179: 3089–107. https://doi.org/10.1007/s11098-022-01854-x.

2022b. 'How to Be Humean About Idealisation Laws'. *Philosophy of Science*, 1–29. https://doi.org/10.1017/psa.2022.12.

'A Structural Equations Approach to Analysing Dispositions'. Unpublished manuscript.

Giannini, Giacomo. 2022. 'Powers, Processes, and Time'. *Erkenntnis* 87: 2801–25. https://doi.org/10.1007/s10670-020-00327-z.

Giannotti, Joaquim. 2021a. 'The Identity Theory of Powers Revised'. *Erkenntnis* 86: 603–21. https://doi.org/10.1007/s10670-019-00122-5.

2021b. 'Pure Powers Are Not Powerful Qualities'. *European Journal of Analytic Philosophy* 17 (1): 2–5. https://doi.org/10.31820/ejap.17.1.2.

Godfrey, Julie. 2020. 'Dispositional Essentialism and Ontic Structural Realism – a Hybrid View'. Ph.D. thesis, Durham University.

Groff, Ruth Porter. 2021. 'Conceptualizing Causal Powers: Activity, Capacity, Essence, Necessitation'. *Synthese* 199: 9881–96. https://doi.org/10.1007/s11229-021-03229-x.

Hájek, Alan. 2020. 'Minkish Dispositions'. *Synthese* 197 (11): 4795–811. https://doi.org/10.1007/s11229-015-1011-y.

Hale, Bob. 2002. 'The Source of Necessity'. *Noûs* 36 (s16): 299–319. https://doi.org/10.1111/1468-0068.36.s16.11.

Halpern, Joseph Y., and Judea Pearl. 2005. 'Causes and Explanations: A Structural-Model Approach. Part I: Causes'. *British Journal for the Philosophy of Science* 56 (4): 843–87. https://doi.org/10.1093/bjps/axi147.

Handfield, Toby. 2010. 'Dispositions, Manifestations, and Causal Structure'. In *The Metaphysics of Powers: Their Grounding and Their Manifestations*, edited by Anna Marmodoro, 106–32. Routledge. https://philarchive.org/rec/HANDMA.

Harre, Rom, and Edward Madden. 1975. *Causal Powers: A Theory of Natural Necessity*. Wiley-Blackwell.

Hauska, Jan. 2015. 'How to Welcome Spontaneous Manifestations'. *Mind* 124 (493): 147–76.

Hawthorne, John. 2002. 'Causal Structuralism'. In *Metaphysics*, edited by James Tomberlin, 361–78. Blackwell.

2005. 'Chance and Counterfactuals'. *Philosophy and Phenomenological Research* 70 (2): 396–405. https://doi.org/10.1111/j.1933-1592.2005.tb00534.x.

Hawthorne, John, and David Manley. 2005. 'Stephen Mumford. Dispositions'. *Noûs* 39 (1): 179–95. https://doi.org/10.1111/j.0029-4624.2005.00499.x.

Heil, John. 2003. *From an Ontological Point of View*. Oxford University Press.

2010. 'Powerful Qualities'. In *The Metaphysics of Powers: Their Grounding and Their Manifestations*, edited by Anna Marmodoro, 58–72. Routledge.

2012. *The Universe as We Find It*. Oxford University Press.

2015. 'III – Aristotelian Supervenience'. *Proceedings of the Aristotelian Society* 115 (1pt1): 41–56.

Hildebrand, Tyler. 2016. 'Two Types of Quidditism'. *Australasian Journal of Philosophy* 94 (3): 516–32. https://doi.org/10.1080/00048402.2015.1112418.

Hitchcock, Christopher. 2001. 'The Intransitivity of Causation Revealed in Equations and Graphs'. *Journal of Philosophy* 98 (6): 273–99. https://doi.org/10.2307/2678432.

Hüttemann, Andreas. 2004. *What's Wrong with Microphysicalism?* Routledge.

Ingthorsson, Rögnvaldur. 2013. 'Properties: Qualities, Powers, or Both?' *Dialectica* 67 (1): 55–80. https://doi.org/10.1111/1746-8361.12011.

Jaag, Siegfried. 2014. 'Dispositional Essentialism and the Grounding of Natural Modality'. *Philosophers' Imprint* 14 (34): 1–21.

Jacobs, Jonathan D. 2010. 'A Powers Theory of Modality: Or, How I Learned to Stop Worrying and Reject Possible Worlds'. *Philosophical Studies* 151 (2): 227–48. https://doi.org/10.1007/s11098-009-9427-1.

2011. 'Powerful Qualities, Not Pure Powers'. *The Monist* 94 (1): 81–102.

ed. 2017. *Causal Powers*. Oxford University Press.

Jenkins, Carrie, and Daniel Nolan. 2012. 'Disposition Impossible'. *Noûs* 46 (4): 732–53.

Johnston, Mark. 1992. 'How to Speak of the Colors'. *Philosophical Studies* 68 (3): 221–63. https://doi.org/10.1007/bf00694847.

Katzav, Joel. 2004. 'Dispositions and the Principle of Least Action'. *Analysis* 64 (3): 206–14. https://doi.org/10.1093/analys/64.3.206.

2005. 'On What Powers Cannot Do'. *Dialectica* 59 (3): 331–45. https://doi.org/10.1111/dltc.2005.59.issue-3.

Kim, Jaegwon. 1998. *Mind in a Physical World: An Essay on the Mind–Body Problem and Mental Causation*. MIT Press.

2000. 'Making Sense of Downward Causation'. In *Downward Causation*, edited by Peter Bøgh Andersen, Claus Emmeche, Niels Ole Finnemann, and Peder Voetmann Christiansen, 305–21. University of Aarhus Press.

Kimpton-Nye, Samuel. 2017. 'Humean Laws in an UnHumean World'. *Journal of the American Philosophical Association* 3 (2): 129–47. https://doi.org/10.1017/apa.2017.19.

2018a. 'Common Ground for Laws and Metaphysical Modality'. Ph.D. thesis, King's College London. https://kclpure.kcl.ac.uk/portal/files/103560842/2018_Kimpton_Nye_Samuel_0812497_ethesis.pdf.

2018b. 'Hardcore Actualism and Possible Non-Existence'. *Thought: A Journal of Philosophy* 7 (2): 122–31. https://doi.org/10.1002/tht3.377.

2020. 'Necessary Laws and the Problem of Counterlegals'. *Philosophy of Science* 87 (3): 518–35. https://doi.org/10.1086/708710.

2021a. 'Can Hardcore Actualism Validate S5?' *Philosophy and Phenomenological Research* 102 (2): 342–58. https://doi.org/10.1111/phpr.12656.

2021b. 'Reconsidering the Dispositional Essentialist Canon'. *Philosophical Studies* 178: 3421–41. https://doi.org/10.1007/s11098-021-01607-2.

2021c. 'The Possibility Bias Is Not Justified'. Unpublished manuscript.

2022a. 'Pandispositionalism and the Metaphysics of Powers'. *Synthese* 200 (5): 371. https://doi.org/10.1007/s11229-022-03857-x.

2022b. 'Laws of Nature: Necessary and Contingent'. *Philosophical Quarterly* 72 (4): 875–95. https://doi.org/10.1093/pq/pqab062.

Kistler, Max. 2010. 'Review of: Alexander Bird, Nature's Metaphysics – Laws and Properties'. *Mind* 119: 188–93.

2012. 'Powerful Properties and the Causal Basis of Dispositions'. In *Properties, Powers, and Structures: Issues in the Metaphysics of Realism*, edited by Alexander Bird, Brian David Ellis, and Howard Sankey, 119–37. Routledge.

2020. 'Powers, Dispositions and Laws of Nature'. In *Dispositionalism: Perspectives from Metaphysics and the Philosophy of Science* (Synthese Library), edited by Anne Sophie Meincke, 171–88. Springer.

Kratzer, Angelika. 1991. 'Modality'. In *Semantics: An International Handbook of Contemporary Research*, edited by Arnim von Stechow and Dieter Wunderlich, 639–50. de Gruyter.

Leech, Jessica. 2017. 'Potentiality'. *Analysis* 77 (2): 457–67. https://doi.org/10.1093/analys/anx047.

Lewis, David. 1973a. 'Causation'. *Journal of Philosophy* 70 (17): 556–67. https://doi.org/10.2307/2025310.

1973b. *Counterfactuals*. Blackwell.

1983. 'New Work for a Theory of Universals'. *Australasian Journal of Philosophy* 61 (4): 343–77. https://doi.org/10.1080/00048408312341131.

1986. *On the Plurality of Worlds*. Basil Blackwell.

1994. 'Humean Supervenience Debugged'. *Mind* 103 (412): 473–90.

1997. 'Finkish Dispositions'. *Philosophical Quarterly (1950–)* 47 (187): 143–58.

2009. 'Ramseyan Humility'. In *Conceptual Analysis and Philosophical Naturalism*, edited by David Braddon-Mitchell and Robert Nola, 203–22. MIT Press.

Locke, Dustin. 2012. 'Quidditism without Quiddities'. *Philosophical Studies* 160 (3): 345–63. https://doi.org/10.1007/s11098-011-9722-5.

Loewer, Barry. 2007. 'Laws and Natural Properties'. *Philosophical Topics* 35 (1/2): 313–28.

Lowe, E. J. 2007. *The Four-Category Ontology: A Metaphysical Foundation for Natural Science*. Oxford University Press.

Manley, David, and Ryan Wasserman. 2007. 'A Gradable Approach to Dispositions'. *Philosophical Quarterly* 57 (226): 68–75. https://doi.org/10.1111/j.1467-9213.2007.469.x.

2008. 'On Linking Dispositions and Conditionals'. *Mind* 117 (465): 59–84. https://doi.org/10.1093/mind/fzn003.

2011. 'Dispositions, Conditionals, and Counterexamples'. *Mind* 120 (480): 1191–1227. https://doi.org/10.1093/mind/fzr078.

Martin, Charles Burton. 1994. 'Dispositions and Conditionals'. *Philosophical Quarterly* 44 (174): 1–8. https://doi.org/10.2307/2220143.

1997. 'On the Need for Properties: The Road to Pythagoreanism and Back'. *Synthese* 112 (2): 193–231.

2007. *The Mind in Nature*. Oxford University Press.

Martin, Charles Burton, and John Heil. 1999. 'The Ontological Turn'. *Midwest Studies in Philosophy* 23 (1): 34–60.

Maudlin, Tim. 2007. *The Metaphysics within Physics*. Oxford University Press.

Mckitrick, Jennifer. 2003. 'The Bare Metaphysical Possibility of Bare Dispositions'. *Philosophy and Phenomenological Research* 66 (2): 349–69. https://doi.org/10.1111/j.1933-1592.2003.tb00265.x.

2010. 'Manifestations as Effects'. In *The Metaphysics of Powers: Their Grounding and Their Manifestations*, edited by Anna Marmodoro, 73–83. Routledge.

2018. *Dispositional Pluralism*. Oxford University Press.

Mellor, David Hugh. 1974. 'In Defense of Dispositions'. *Philosophical Review* 83 (2): 157–81. https://doi.org/10.2307/2184136.

1982. 'Counting Corners Correctly'. *Analysis* 42 (2): 96–97. https://doi.org/10.1093/analys/42.2.96.

1995. *The Facts of Causation*. Routledge.

Molnar, George. 2003. *Powers: A Study in Metaphysics*. Oxford University Press.

Mumford, Stephen. 1998. *Dispositions*. Clarendon Press.

2004. *Laws in Nature*. 1st ed. Routledge.

2006. 'The Ungrounded Argument'. *Synthese* 149 (3): 471–89.

2021. 'Where the Real Power Lies: A Reply to Bird'. *Mind* 130 (520): 1295–1308. https://doi.org/10.1093/mind/fzab046.

Mumford, Stephen, and Rani Lill Anjum. 2011. *Getting Causes from Powers*. Oxford University Press.

Nolan, Daniel. 2015. 'Noncausal Dispositions'. *Noûs* 49 (3): 425–39. https://doi.org/10.1111/nous.12096.

Paoletti, Michele Paolini. 2021. 'Masks, Interferers, Finks, and Mimickers: A Novel Approach'. *Theoria* 87 (3): 813–36. https://doi.org/10.1111/theo.12318.

Pearl, Judea. 2000. *Causality: Models, Reasoning and Inference*. Cambridge University Press.

Prior, Elizabeth W. 1985. *Dispositions*. Humanities Press.

Prior, Elizabeth W., Robert Pargetter, and Frank Jackson. 1982. 'Three Theses about Dispositions'. *American Philosophical Quarterly* 19 (3): 251–57.

Psillos, Stathis. 2006a. 'The Structure, the Whole Structure, and Nothing but the Structure?' *Philosophy of Science* 73 (5): 560–70. https://doi.org/10.1086/518326.

2006b. 'What Do Powers Do When They Are Not Manifested?' *Philosophy and Phenomenological Research* 72 (1): 137–56.

Quine, Willard Van Orman. 1948. 'On What There Is'. *Review of Metaphysics* 2 (5): 21–38.

1970. 'Natural Kinds'. In *Essays in Honor of Carl G. Hempel*, edited by Nicholas Rescher, 5. D. Reidel.

1974. *The Roots of Reference*. Open Court.

Rodriguez-Pereyra, Gonzalo. 2015. 'Grounding Is Not a Strict Order'. *Journal of the American Philosophical Association* 1 (3): 517–34.

Russell, Bertrand. 1912. 'On the Notion of Cause'. *Proceedings of the Aristotelian Society* 13: 1–26.

Ryle, Gilbert. 1949. *The Concept of Mind*. Hutchinson & Co.

Schaffer, Jonathan. 2004. 'Two Conceptions of Sparse Properties*'. *Pacific Philosophical Quarterly* 85 (1): 92–102. https://doi.org/10.1111/j.1468-0114.2004.00189.x.

2005. 'Quidditistic Knowledge'. *Philosophical Studies* 123 (1–2): 1–32. https://doi.org/10.1007/s11098-004-5221-2.

2016a. 'Grounding in the Image of Causation'. *Philosophical Studies* 173 (1): 49–100.

2016b. 'It Is the Business of Laws to Govern'. *Dialectica* 70 (4): 577–88. https://doi.org/10.1111/1746-8361.12165.

2017. 'The Ground between the Gaps'. *Philosopher's Imprint* 17 (11). http://hdl.handle.net/2027/spo.3521354.0017.011.

Schrenk, Markus. 2017. *The Metaphysics of Science: A Systematic and Historical Introduction*. Routledge.

Schwitzgebel, Eric. 2002. 'A Phenomenal, Dispositional Account of Belief'. *Noûs* 36 (2): 249–75.

Sider, Theodore. 2020. *The Tools of Metaphysics and the Metaphysics of Science*. Oxford University Press.

Smart, Benjamin T. H., and Karim P. Y. Thébault. 2015. 'Dispositions and the Principle of Least Action Revisited'. *Analysis* 75 (3): 386–95. https://doi.org/10.1093/analys/anv050.

Smith, Deborah C. 2016. 'Quid Quidditism Est?' *Erkenntnis* 81 (2): 237–57. https://doi.org/10.1007/s10670-015-9737-y.

Smith, Michael, David Lewis, and Mark Johnston. 1989. 'Dispositional Theories of Value'. *Proceedings of the Aristotelian Society, Supplementary Volumes* 63: 89–174.

Steinberg, Jesse R. 2010. 'Dispositions and Subjunctives'. *Philosophical Studies* 148 (3): 323–41. https://doi.org/10.1007/s11098-008-9325-y.

Storer, T. 1951. 'On Defining "Soluble"'. *Analysis* 11 (6): 134–7. https://doi.org/10.1093/analys/11.6.134.

Taylor, Henry. 2018. 'Powerful Qualities and Pure Powers'. *Philosophical Studies* 175 (6): 1423–40. https://doi.org/10.1007/s11098-017-0918-1.

2022. 'Powerful Problems for Powerful Qualities'. *Erkenntnis* 87: 425–33. https://doi.org/10.1007/s10670-019-00199-y.

Thompson, Naomi. 2016. 'Metaphysical Interdependence'. In *Reality Making*, edited by Mark Jago, 38–56. Oxford University Press.

Tooley, Michael. 1977. 'The Nature of Laws'. *Canadian Journal of Philosophy* 7 (4): 667–98.

Trogdon, Kelly. 2013. 'Grounding: Necessary or Contingent?' *Pacific Philosophical Quarterly* 94 (4): 465–85.

Tugby, Matthew. 2012. 'Rescuing Dispositionalism from the Ultimate Problem: Reply to Barker and Smart'. *Analysis* 72 (4): 723–31.

2013. 'Platonic Dispositionalism'. *Mind* 122 (486): 451–80.

2021. 'Grounding Theories of Powers'. *Synthese* 198 (12): 11187–216. https://doi.org/10.1007/s11229-020-02781-2.

2022a. *Putting Properties First: A Platonic Metaphysics for Natural Modality*. Oxford University Press.

2022b. 'Dispositional Realism without Dispositional Essences'. *Synthese* 200 (3): 222. https://doi.org/10.1007/s11229-022-03554-9.

Vetter, Barbara. 2011a. 'On Linking Dispositions and Which Conditionals?' *Mind* 120 (480): 1173–89. https://doi.org/10.1093/mind/fzr077.

2011b. 'Recent Work: Modality without Possible Worlds'. *Analysis* 71 (4): 742–54. https://doi.org/10.1093/analys/anr077.

2012. 'Dispositional Essentialism and the Laws of Nature'. In *Properties, Powers and Structures. Issues in the Metaphysics of Realism*, edited by Alexander Bird, Brian Ellis, and Howard Sankey, 201–16. Routledge.

2014. 'Dispositions without Conditionals'. *Mind* 123 (489): 129–56. https://doi.org/10.1093/mind/fzu032.

2015. *Potentiality: From Dispositions to Modality*. 1st ed. Oxford Philosophical Monographs. Oxford University Press.

2018. 'II – Evolved Powers, Artefact Powers, and Dispositional Explanations'. *Aristotelian Society Supplementary Volume* 92 (1): 277–97. https://doi.org/10.1093/arisup/aky007.

2020. 'Replies'. *Philosophical Inquiries* 8 (1): 199–222. https://doi.org/10.4454/philinq.v8i1.282.

2021. 'Explanatory Dispositionalism'. *Synthese* 199: 2051–75. https://doi.org/10.1007/s11229-020-02872-0.

Vetter, Barbara, and Ralf Busse. 2022. 'Modal Dispositionalism and Necessary Perfect Masks'. *Analysis* 82 (1): 84–94. https://doi.org/10.1093/analys/anab061.

Vogt, Lisa. 2022. 'Nominalist Dispositional Essentialism'. *Synthese* 200 (2): 156. https://doi.org/10.1007/s11229-022-03588-z.

Wang, Jennifer. 2015. 'The Modal Limits of Dispositionalism'. *Noûs* 49 (3): 454–69.

Wasserman, Ryan. 2011. 'Dispositions and Generics'. *Philosophical Perspectives* 25 (1): 425–53. https://doi.org/10.1111/j.1520-8583.2011.00223.x.

Whittle, Ann. 2009. 'Causal Nominalism'. In *Dispositions and Causes*, edited by Toby Handfield, 242–85. Oxford University Press.

Wildman, Nathan. 2020. 'Potential Problems? Some Issues with Vetter's Potentiality Account of Modality'. *Philosophical Inquiries* 8 (1): 167–84. https://doi.org/10.4454/philinq.v8i1.280.

Williams, Neil E. 2011. 'Dispositions and the Argument From Science'. *Australasian Journal of Philosophy* 89 (1): 71–90. https://doi.org/10.1080/00048400903527766.

2019. *The Powers Metaphysic*. Oxford University Press.

Williamson, Timothy. 2007. *The Philosophy of Philosophy*. Wiley-Blackwell.

2013. *Modal Logic as Metaphysics*. Oxford University Press.

Wilson, Alastair. 2018. 'Metaphysical Causation'. *Noûs* 52 (4): 723–51. https://doi.org/10.1111/nous.12190.

Wilson, Jessica M. 2010. 'What Is Hume's Dictum, and Why Believe It?' *Philosophy and Phenomenological Research* 80 (3): 595–637.

Woodward, James. 2003. *Making Things Happen: A Theory of Causal Explanation*. Oxford University Press.

Yalowitz, Steven. 2000. 'A Dispositional Account of Self-Knowledge'. *Philosophy and Phenomenological Research* 61 (2): 249–78. https://doi.org/10.2307/2653651.

Yates, David. 2015. 'Dispositionalism and the Modal Operators'. *Philosophy and Phenomenological Research* 91 (2): 411–24.

2016. 'Is Powerful Causation an Internal Relation?' In *The Metaphysics of Relations*, edited by Anna Marmodoro and David Yates, 138–56. Oxford University Press.

2018. 'Inverse Functionalism and the Individuation of Powers'. *Synthese* 195: 4525–50.

Acknowledgements

We'd like the thank Max Kistler and Matthew Tugby for their very helpful comments on an initial draft of this book. The research for this book was funded by the European Research Council (ERC) under the European Union's (EU) Horizon 2020 research and innovation programme, grant agreement No 771509 ('MetaScience').

Cambridge Elements

Metaphysics

Tuomas E. Tahko
University of Bristol

Tuomas E. Tahko is Professor of Metaphysics of Science at the University of Bristol, UK. Tahko specializes in contemporary analytic metaphysics, with an emphasis on methodological and epistemic issues: 'meta-metaphysics'. He also works at the interface of metaphysics and philosophy of science: 'metaphysics of science'. Tahko is the author of *Unity of Science* (Cambridge University Press, 2021, *Elements in Philosophy of Science*), *An Introduction to Metametaphysics* (Cambridge University Press, 2015) and editor of *Contemporary Aristotelian Metaphysics* (Cambridge University Press, 2012).

About the Series

This highly accessible series of Elements provides brief but comprehensive introductions to the most central topics in metaphysics. Many of the Elements also go into considerable depth, so the series will appeal to both students and academics. Some Elements bridge the gaps between metaphysics, philosophy of science, and epistemology.

Cambridge Elements ≡

Metaphysics

Elements in the Series

A full series listing is available at: www.cambridge.org/EMPH